Sidney Ploss is a Russia scholar and historian. He holds a BA from Syracuse University and a PhD from London University. He taught at the University of Pennsylvania.

In memory of Hugh Seton-Watson.

Sidney Ploss

Russia in History

A Concise Survey of Policies

Austin Macauley Publishers™
London • Cambridge • New York • Sharjah

Ordering Information:
Quantity sales: special discounts are available on quantity purchases by corporations, associations, and others. For details, contact the publisher at the address below.

Publisher's Cataloging-in-Publication data
Ploss, Sidney
Russia in History: A Concise Survey of Policies

ISBN 9781643784960 (Paperback)
ISBN 9781643784977 (Hardback)
ISBN 9781645367963 (ePub e-book)

Library of Congress Control Number: 2019907839

The main category of the book — History / Russia & the Former Soviet Union

www.austinmacauley.com/us

First Published (2019)
Austin Macauley Publishers LLC
40 Wall Street, 28th Floor
New York, NY 10005
USA
mail-usa@austinmacauley.com
+1 (646) 5125767

I gratefully recognize the diligence of the editorial and production staff at Austin Macauley Publishers.

Table of Contents

"With a doctrinaire dogmatism, Russians at all times blend shrewd realistic perception. Devoid, or free, of the roman tradition and untainted with modern bourgeois conventions, Russia follows a path of her own and pursues policy which is logical and clear-sighted if viewed from the angle of its own premises, devious and incomprehensible when correlated to conceptions alien to it."

Historian Sir Lewis B. Namier

"The future is a land of which there are no maps; and historians err when they describe even the most purposeful stated as though he were marching down a broad high road with his objective already in sight. More flexible historians admit that a statesman often has alternative courses before him; yet even they deploy him as choosing the route at a crossroads? Certainly, the development of history has its own logical ideas. But these laws resemble rather than those by which floodwater flows into hitherto unseen channels and forces itself finally to an unpredictable sea."

Historian A. J. Taylor

"If one looks back at the history of this country, one can see that, at any time, from one day to the next, the most unexpected things can happen…"

German Ambassador to the USSR Count Schulenburg

Preface

Opinions differ on the traits and motives of Russian leaders. Insecure and destructive is one conclusion. Too dependent on reports of intelligence officers is another. A third view is that a new Russian Empire is under construction. A Russian intellectual muses that perhaps each side, in Washington and Moscow, lacks the analytical ability to judge the capacity of the other side.

We ask the question: In which direction is Russia evolving? Where it is now is suggested in a Note on Post-Soviet Russia. What follows is an outline history of Russia and the USSR. It is offered with an assumption that usually the pattern of a nation's development gives a clue to its future.

Our emphasis is on the crucial nature of leadership initiatives in the unfolding of Russian history. One scholar warns against personalizing history since other leaders could have reached similar conclusions. A like-thinking colleague spotlighted modernization and evaluated Stalin as a generic symptom of accelerating modernity, rather than a unique individual to be judged on his personal merits.

Sir Bernard Pares was an eyewitness to the 1917 revolution in Russia. He admonished the abstractionists in an examination of turning points. Theories of inevitability should be avoided, and direct observers are often more reliable sources. This tallies with an observation of Michael Florinsky, who wrote the best single work on Russian history, that "careful consideration has led me to the conclusion that the personalities of the tsars and emperors had a greater part in determining the course of Russian history than I was at first inclined to believe."

I am indebted to the scholarship of Russian historians Vasili Kliuchevsky, Alexander Kornilov, Sergei Platonov, and George Vernadsky. No less penetrating have been the works of Western specialists Michael Florinsky, Roberta Manning, Evan Mawdsley, Hugh Seton-Watson, and Benedict Sumner.

Chapter I

Building a Nation-State

Land and People

Summary

In a series of epic migrations across Eurasia, Russians thirsted for adventure or social justice. They found much adversity, natural and otherwise, which made them tough. Evidence for this assumption about national character initially dates to ancient and medieval events beyond the earlier migrations.

Russia was semi-barbaric as Europe advanced beyond the Middle Ages (300–1500). A political map of multiple power centers took shape. Moscow princes forcibly gained ascendance under Mongol supremacy (1240–1480). The Greek Orthodox Church brought rudiments of culture and arts.

A striking feature of Old Russia was recurrent warfare. Asiatic and Turkic bands repeatedly stormed into the few towns, devastating most and creating a sea of ragged villagers. Civil strife among rival princes was another obstacle to progress. The Russian garrison state, accordingly, was an upshot of challenge and expansionism over centuries.

***

Ancient Russia stretched from the Carpathian Mountains in the west to the Upper Volga River in the east. The distant horizon in much of the great plain of Western Russia has struck some as a factor behind the inhabitants' maximalist and catastrophic thoughts. Historian Evan Mawdsley notes that "European Russia is not the endless grassy plain of the 'steppe.' Its territory is divided into three vegetation belts. Thick forests are common in the north, further south there is wooded steppe, and only south to the Black Sea does the steppe proper open out." It has been usual to stress Russia's immensity, absence of naturally defensive frontiers and vulnerability to attacks from many sides. As a result, society became ripe for one-man rule along military lines. But Russia's vastness could be a strategic asset as well. Vladimir Lenin, architect of the Soviet system, in 1918 raised the "possibility of holding out during a comparatively long civil war, partly thanks to the gigantic size of the country and in the bad means of communications." Lenin deputy Leon Trotsky added, "If we are alive today as an independent and revolutionary country… this is due to our expanses." World War II historian Chester Wilmot pointed out that armies advancing into Russia out of the narrow throat between the Baltic and Black Sea were soon swallowed up in the extent of the steppes. Paul Kennedy tells us that strategic depth acutely hurt German invaders in 1941: "The sheer geographical extent and logistical demands of campaigning hundreds of miles deep into Russia undermined the Wehrmacht's greatest advantage: its ability to launch shock attacks within limited confines, so as to overwhelm the enemy before its own supplies begin to run out and its war machine slowed down."

Severe weather conditions have slowed or benefited armies on Russian soil. Spring and autumn rain and mud seasons alternated with deep snowdrifts in sub-zero temperatures. The Russian climate had to impact psychology. Variations as frost in August induced peasants to be cautious. And, like other northerners, Russians were drawn to alcohol, which became a national scourge.

The main rivers of Russia helped to shape migration and trade patterns. Volga, Dnieper, and Western Dvina flowed into the Caspian, Black and Baltic Seas, respectively; the Volga was extolled in song as Mother of Rivers. The waterway formed by the Neva, Lake Ladoga and the Volkhov, Lake Ilmen, and the Lovat spilled into the Gulf of Finland. To the east, the Kama River is near the Ob in Western Siberia, which enabled runaway slaves and serfs known as Cossacks (a Tatar word for "light horseman") to roam beyond the Ural hills that are assumed to separate Europe and Asia.

Before the Christian era, Iranian and Greek states thrived around the Black Sea. After their demise in the 370s, the Hums, Mongolians known as the Hsiung-Hu, moved through south Russia into the Balkans. Goths from Europe created an empire in Russia during the 500s.

Over the course of 1,000 years, the southern steppes of Russia were a battleground. Goths replaced Huns, Huns–

Averis, Averis–Ugrians and Khazars–Pechenegs, Khazars–Pechenegs–Polovetsians. The Polovetsians–Tatars controlled the great plain and northern forest.

During the invasions, Slavic and Finnish tribes comparable to the Iroquois in North America lived in huts near future towns and called themselves Poliane (Kiev), Severian (Chernigov), Radamichi (Liubech), Krivichi (Smolensk and Poletsk), and Ilmen (Novgorod). Family groups merged into tribes, and their communes shunned personal property. In time, princes and clan elders ruled through public meetings.

Stages of Russian internal colonization were defined in the lectures of Imperial historian Vasili Kliuchevsky:

1. 700s to 1200s: movement from the southwest to the middle and upper Dnieper (Kievan era)
2. 1200s to 1400s: Upper Volga principalities and estates with free labor.
3. 1400s to 1600s: Moscow tsars gather in lands to the south and east, to the Black Soil belt in the mid-Volga; serfdom introduced.
4. 1600s to 1800s: a Russian Empire from the Baltic to the White Sea, Caucasus mountains, Caspian Sea and Urals; migrants to Little Russia (Ukraine), White Russia and New Russia, along the Black Sea coast.

Kliuchevsky estimated the arrival of two million Russians in Siberia from 1907–09 by a new transcontinental railroad.

Norse Vikings founded a state at Kiev in the 9th century. They were known as Rus, and Orthodox chronicles affirm that local Slavs invited the Vikings to bring social order. Historian Norman Cantor saw Russia as a haven for Viking war bands expelled after defeats in battles in Denmark and Norway. Their level of culture was that of primitive German tribes that invaded Western Europe in the 5th and 6th centuries. Vikings were pirates and known to drown tyrannical rulers in wells.

Riurik, a Norse Viking, is likely to have seized power in the northern trade center of Novgorod around 862. Until the mid-1200s, Kiev on the Dnieper was the "Mother of Russian Cities." It united tribes and towns of the southern borderlands. War and trade with the Byzantine Empire highlighted the reigns or Viking grand princes Oleg and Igor (879–945). The first Kievan ruler with a Slavic name was Sviatoslav (964–73). To conquer lands rich in gold, silver, wine, and horses, he led campaigns to the Volga and Caspian, fought against Byzantium; and met death at the hands of the Asiatic Pechenegs.

Honored today in Russia and Ukraine as patron saint is Vladimir, grand prince of Kievan Russia (978–1015). He was enthroned after defeating in combat his brothers, Yaropolk and Oleg. Vladimir was baptized in 988 and forcibly "converted" Russia. Greek Orthodox clergy from Byzantium taught the basics of the new faith and exalted Russia's ruler as God's representative on earth. The Church would play a leading role in Russian literature, art, and music. Miracle worker icons were carried to battlefields in the 16th century. The eastern Catholic church also sowed distrust of Western Europe as a source of papal heresy.

Sobernost or Godly communal life was valued and individualism deplored.

Russia's conversion entailed a long struggle with pagan cults which venerated nature and ancestors. The dead were thought to be wandering the earth and inhabiting fields, forest, and waters. In the 19th century, pagan holidays were observed and featured much revelry. The German traveler Jens Muhling reports that in 2010, he saw a Slavic pagan rite in a Russian village called Popovka; youthful settlers adopted the old faith during Mikhail Gorbachev's reform era.

In Kievan politics, the Christian tenets were ignored. Civil wars and fratricides were common to settle disputes over royal succession. Grand prince Sviatopolk killed three brothers and was called The Damned before he fell in 1019. Once fathers and sons perished, uncles and nephews dueled. Historian M. P. Pogodin estimated that 80 years of fratricidal war occurred in a span of 170 years (1055–1225). This strife, nomadic raids, and shifts in East-West trade routes led to population flight from Kiev.

The basic institutions and social structure of Kievan Russia were reproduced in quieter northern areas. A grand prince served as commander-in-chief, magistrate, and tax collector. He owned slaves and villages, where wives, daughters, and monasteries were to be found. One such potentate, Andrey Boqoliubsky, prince of Vladimir–Suzdal, who sacked Kiev in 1169, was notoriously stern, capricious, and lacking self-control. He was killed in a plot of aristocrats (1174).

The grand prince's druzhina or retinue was a coterie of warriors and advisers. Boyars were the most illustrious figures and in the Moscow state recognized as the upper aristocracy. Below were tax clerks and soldiers.

In Novgorod, a town assembly (veche) ratified policies and sometimes overruled the monarch or ousted him. A bell was rung to convene the veche and silenced when the city fell to Moscow in 1471.

The social divisions in Kiev were observed elsewhere:

1. The public (liudi)
2. Aristocrats (boyary)
3. Peasants (krestiane)
4. Slaves (raby or kholopy)
5. Church people (tserkovniki, i.e., bishops, priests, monks, servants, infirm, rightless, and slaves).

The Kievan economy was diverse and its ties extended to Europe. Princes and boyars lived on large estates with much livestock. Incomes of owners and tenants derived from hunting, fishing, and bee keeping. Weavers made clothing, and merchant corporations handled foreign trade with Bohemia and Germany. The exports were furs, flax, silverware, wine, silk, and glassware. Eastern imports included jewels and steel weapons. The trading quarter of Kiev situated the businesses of Germans, Armenians, and Jews. A law code (1164) regulated corporate business.

Ivan Kalita became grand prince of Moscow in 1328. His dynasty took deep root during all but three years, the grand princedom remained with the direct descendants of Ivan until 1598. Within the new stone fortifications of the Kremlin, the Kalitas endured foreign sieges and civil wars. A review of Moscow's battles from 1372 to 1613, when a

300-year dynasty began, shows 16 wars and civil wars. Six wars were fought against Tatars, who burned Moscow in 1382 and 1521. Lithuanians and Swedes were major antagonists, as were Polish interventionists. Alliances were made with other regions (Nizhni–Novgorod, Yaroslavl, Novgorod, Tver, and Pskov) which were absorbed into the centralized Moscow state. The gentry forced peasants into serfdom.

Ivan Ill (1462–1505) was proclaimed "Sovereign of All Russia," and the whole country declared his hereditary estate Architect of the Russian police state, Ivan detected a plot in occupied Novgorod and executed 150 local boyars. Their property was confiscated, and a transfer of upper-class persons was decreed: 8,000 families were sent to Moscow, and the same number of Muscovite families ordered to Novgorod. The middle classes were also resettled to break local ties. Most of the Novgorod church land was later granted to Moscow officials and army officers.

Ivan Ill was a vocal Russian nationalist and mythmaker. He claimed ownership of all lands in historic memory that were Russian. The Viking Riurik, credited with starting the first dynasty in Kiev, was held to share a bloodline with Caesar Augustus. Kliuchevsky opines: "In those days, people did not think with the use of ideas but with symbols, rituals, and legends. Ideas were not developed logically but in symbolic actions and assumed facts, for which justification was sought in history. People turned to the past not to explain current events, but to justify current interests, seeking examples to legitimize their personal ambitions. The falsehoods grew habitual, developed logically, but in symbolic actions and assumed facts, for which justification was sought in history. People turned to the past not to explain current events but to justify current interests, seeking examples to legitimize their personal ambitions."

To deter revolts and separatism, the son of Ivan Ill, Vasili Ill, seized Pskov (510) and Riazan (1517). Hundreds of local families were sent to Moscow and replaced with Muscovites. Deposed princes served under Vasili as boyars, without hereditary estates. The grumbling of one fallen prince led to a loss of his tongue.

In the meantime, the eastern and southern borders of Moscow were exposed to raids by Turks from Kazan and Crimea. The international prestige of Moscow rose with ties to Poland, Sweden, Germanic knights, and emperors. Trade relations with England were mutually beneficial and verged on political alliance.

The surge of Moscow's power is variously explained. One view is that the political ambition of the grand princes coincided with social pressure for a rallying of the nation against foreign enemies. Others think that Moscow gained an edge by exploiting geographic location, skillful leadership, and Church goodwill.

Marxist historian M. N. Pokrovsky wrote that some Russian monarchs belonged in the criminal division of an insane asylum. He would have included in that pack Ivan IV, the Terrible, born 1530, and reigned 1533–84. He was a contemporary of Henry VIII of England and shared with him virtues and vices. Ivan was pious and fond of biblical maxims. Despite a troubled youth, he was a bold thinker and one of the best read of educated men. He did not assume power until 1547, after his Greek mother served as regent; gossip had it that she was poisoned.

Over the next decades, the law code was reformed, and Kazan, stronghold of Tatar raiders on the Volga, was captured. At the mouth of the Volga, the trading town of Astrakhan was taken. Wars against Poland and Sweden dragged on to the end of Ivan's reign.

Remarkably, Ivan's Kazan triumph had a negative effect. Many peasants migrated from the north to the rich, black-soil areas of the middle and lower Volga. The estates of nobles became unproductive. Decrees restricted freedom of movement. State agents used torture, robbery, and chains to keep peasants on their native turf.

A new wrinkle was Ivan the Terrible's campaign of terror, the oprichnina (1565–72). Prince Andrei Kurbsky began a literary debate with Ivan from his self-imposed exile in Poland–Lithuania. He argued in a letter and book that a Russian leader had to consult on policy with his Boyar Council and National Assembly. Kurbsky protested the holding of secretive state conclaves to which few were invited. Ivan disputed the right of boyars to choose candidates for succession to the grand princedom. A 15-year war of words between the throne and Kurbsky ensued along these lines.

Soon, Ivan established a new governing class. Boyars and clergy were denounced as corrupt and treasonous. An abdication was threatened to test elite loyalties. Delegates to a conference of aristocrats and clergy were stunned when Ivan attacked them as criminals. They pleaded to remain in charge, but Ivan demanded a police dictatorship.

The oprichnina or tsar's personal domain was to exceed in power the zemshchina or state administration. Boyars could run provinces under Ivan's special Court, which was to operate with its own officials and 6,000 more policemen. Clothed in black, the mounted police had dogs' heads and brooms attached to their saddles to assert the right to sniff out and sweep away disloyal subjects. They deported thousands of officials to remote areas and reputedly killed 400 to 10,000 suspects. The metropolitan, Filipp, and Ivan's son were among the victims of the tsar's suspicion. Russian historians have indicted Ivan as intolerant, egotistical, and vindictive. The public, however, chose to remember Ivan as heroic victor over the Tatars at Kazan.

The throne of Kalita passed to Feodor in 1584. His mental disability required the enlistment of Boris Godunov, the tsar's brother-in-law, as Lord Protector or chancellor. A National Assembly in 1598 was packed with Godunov men who elected Boris tsar.

The policies of Godunov were supportive of nationalist and aristocratic interests. Russian influence expanded into the Caucasus and western Siberia. The tsar negotiated creation of a nativist patriarchate to rival one in Jerusalem and he chose a client as top Orthodox prelate. Michael Florinsky says of Boris' policies on the peasant question that he "favored the advancement of serfdom, contributed to the growth of discontent among the masses, and thus prepared his downfall."

A famine stalked in 1601–02 and ushered in civil wars. The Time of Troubles had begun. When Boris died in 1605, pretenders claiming to be Dmitri, son of Ivan the Terrible, who died mysteriously, proclaimed themselves tsar. Poland backed the imposters. In the confusion, Prince Vasili Shuisky was enthroned in 1606 and espoused legality. A special police court was abolished. Boyars had to be queried before a death sentence was passed. The persecution of entire families of State enemies was outlawed. Cases of alleged espionage had to be investigated and liars punished. The peasants were restless and some rebelled. The Poles entered Moscow, overthrew Shuisky, and their Crown Prince Vladislav became tsar (1610).

Russia was driven to the edge of collapse. Criminal and rebel gangs rode across the country, pillaging estates, towns and churches. A national resistance was mounted, and Moscow re-conquered from the Poles.

The Orthodox Church was instrumental in saving Russia from atomization. Patriarch Hermogen was moral leader against foreign meddlers. Bishop Dionosy funded anti-Polish militias. Mikhail Romanov, a teenage nephew of the last tsar of the 300-year-old dynasty was elected tsar in 1613 by a National Assembly. The House of Romanov was alleged to stand over the next three centuries. In fact, German blood through marital ties and cultural interests long prevailed at the throne. More broadly, the new Romanov dynasty was handed a legacy of backwardness – economic, political, and military – that it would not overcome. Assemblies in Europe were easing the tensions between monarchs and aristocrats. Russian assemblies were rallies to mobilize elites and verify their performance. Thus, a road to representative government was blocked. Absent was an understanding of constitutions for defining State structure and civic duties. Half of the Russian nation lived outside the imperial borders. Given the restorational teaching of Ivan Ill, this presaged wars of “liberation” with Poles, Swedes, and Turks.

Chapter II

Holy Russia Divided

Religious Crises

Summary

Christianity was imposed on Russian pagans, and its practice entrusted to Greek clergy from Byzantium. Once the Kievan state atomized, Muscovy became the center of Church life in the 14th century. It enjoyed wild success with the upper classes, and a church-building boom ensued.

Doctrinal fights preoccupied the clergy until a Church Council in 1503 stamped heretical a “no property” belief. Jointly, the hierarchy provided moral and financial leadership to save Russia from atomization during the Time of Troubles.

Ivan the Terrible gained Church support for his drive to centralize governance. A Great Schism arose during his reign, highlighted by the emergence of Old Believers, archconservative Orthodox (1654). Revolts and suicides were common until Peter the Great harnessed the Church to his State machine. Ultimately, nihilists and revolutionaries benefited from the losses of Church and State.

***

The glamor of Byzantium awed the Kievan Princess Olga, who visited Constantinople (957). Her grandson Vladimir, grand prince of Kiev, was baptized and "converted" Russia by fire and sword in 988. The Orthodox Church bolted from the Catholic Church (1054). Secular politics tore apart Orthodoxy. A Council of Florence welcomed reunion of eastern and western Churches. Metropolitan Isidore was deposed in 1441 for acceptance of Florence.

A trio of factions sprang up to heated debate. Trans-Volga Elders exalted spiritualism and apartness from the State. Judaizers rejected icon worship and Church property, including slaves. Josephites favored reliance on State power and wealth. A Church Council in 1504 blessed the Josephites and urged the burning of heretical foes. The outcome of this struggle propelled Orthodoxy on to great wealth. Its monasteries controlled many villages that were taxed and serviced autocratic landowners. This trend put Orthodoxy in the crosshairs of insurgents and brigands.

In the meantime, Orthodoxy was a dynamic of cultural progress. Greek and Serbian ecclesiastics brought to Russia education, literature and the arts. A Bulgarian disciple of St. Cyril and St. Methodius, apostles to the Slavs, devised a written language for Russians. The literary language was Church Slavonic, which blended with Old Russian in ordinary Kievan speech. Churches and holy sites were created in medieval Kiev and elsewhere to glorify God and ancestors. A glance at the church-building drive indicates the piety and pride of Russian Christendom:

1045–57:	Santa Sofia, Kiev, begun
1051:	Founding of the Monastery of the Caves at Kiev
1158:	Beginning of Uspensky Cathedral in Vladimir
1193–97:	Building of St. Dmitri, Vladimir
1397:	Foundation of Byelozero monastery
1436:	Foundation of Solovetsky monastery at the White Sea.

Inside the holy places, the clergy organized choral music and iconography in accord with Byzantine custom. A downside of Church life was very narrow devotion to the words of Jesus.

Neglected were European advances in geometry and astronomy as navigation aids, philosophy, rhetoric, and Latin for the study of classical texts.

Politically, Orthodoxy was solidly behind Ivan the Terrible's push for centralized Muscovite rule. Varied regional saints were merged with new ones into a single Church calendar. The tsar, however, failed to implement his edict barring the clergy from enlarging their land-ownings without his approval. Ivan deposed and murdered the Metropolitan Filipp (1569).

The issues of the Great Schism are totally strange indeed. Whether to make the sign of the cross with two fingers or three; how to spell the name of Jesus; in which direction a Church procession should go, with reference to the sun, the number of hallelujahs to be exclaimed in praise of God. Seeking an explanation of the arguments, Kliuchevsky theorizes that the local conservatives, who called themselves Old Believers, were like poetry lovers who would strongly object to their enchanting verses being translated into prose. Other students of Russian history attribute the devotion to habit a sign of public inertia or ignorance and narrow view of Christianity.

Significantly, a different religious picture was painted in Little Russia. This region, south of Muscovy, was also known as Ukraine or "at the border." There, ethno politics spawned a new variety of Orthodoxy: The Uniate Church, which later fueled Ukrainian nationalism.

Poland and Lithuania in 1569 agreed to incorporate Ukraine into Poland. Jesuits and Polish lords, in 1596, created the Uniate Church as a weapon against Orthodoxy. The new faith was to keep for the Orthodox their rituals but accept the Papacy. Russian bishops who joined the Uniate movement persecuted Orthodox loyalists, seizing property and desecrating graves. The tsar decreed a crackdown on Uniates after the 1863 revolt against Russian rule in Ukraine.

Eastern prelates stoked the fires of debate in the 1640s. The patriarch of Jerusalem visited Moscow and created fear of heresy in Church and State by harping on local deviations. A Russian monk sent to Athens learned that Greek clergy were burning Moscow texts as heretical.

Patriarch Nikon was born Nikita in 1605 into a peasant family in the province of Nizhni- Novgorod. His mother died soon after the birth, and a guardian handled the boy roughly. As a teenager, he learned reading at a monastery and became a village priest at age 20. After the death of his children, Nikita went to a monastery near the White Sea, clashed with the abbot, and went to Moscow. There he became intimate with Patriarch Joseph, who got him named head of the New Jerusalem monastery outside the capital.

The royal Romanovs were entombed at New Jerusalem, and Nikita stuck up a friendship with Tsar Aleksei Romanov, 25 years younger and impressed by the cleric's golden tongue. Ahead for Nikita – thanks to networking – was his appointment as Metropolitan of Novgorod. There, he won popularity as source of order and famine relief.

In 1648, the tsar sided with gentry and had a National Assembly narrow the land ownership and judicial rights of the Church. Nikita denounced with extreme asperity the 1649 Law Code establishing limits to clerical authority. He persuaded the tsar to overturn the antichurch rulings. Moreover, the Assembly was never recalled, and only after the 1905 Revolution was a half-parliament introduced.

In 1652, Nikita was the tsar's choice to succeed Joseph as patriarch. The nominee agreed to serve only if the tsar, boyars and prelates swore to obey him as Initiator (nachalnik) "in everything." That was done and, as Nikon, the peasant-son Nikita was recognized as Majesty or co-tsar.

Nikon read the charter of the patriarchate and learned that he had to maintain Church unity against disruptive innovations. It is conceivable that political as well as dogmatic motive lurked behind Nikon's crusade against the Old Believers. Moscow officials may have thought that aligning the haphazard services with the proper Ukrainian ones could make it easier for southerners to accept a controversial tsarist protectorate over their land. (Kiev and Ukraine would be ceded by Poland to Moscow in 1667.) Moscow perhaps hoped, too, that Kievan prelates would switch their loyalty from the patriarch of Constantinople to the Moscow patriarch if the reforms were enacted.

Change began with reduction from 12 to 4 the number of genuflections made during the reading or a prayer in praise of God. Moscow priests wrote to the tsar that Nikon was guilty of a heresy. Some of them were arrested and sent to Siberia. A protesting bishop was banished after a 1654 Church Council mandated new revisions. Hundreds of old religious books were collected in the east and sent to Moscow for guidance of editors. A certain Arseni the Greek was a prospective editor who had studied in Rome and Venice. Rumor had it that he was a Catholic heretic. He was sent to the monastery in the Solovetsky Islands for evaluation by monks. Three years later, Arseni was cleared as genuine Orthodox and fit to rectify holy writ.

In spite of public resistance, Nikon pressed ahead. A Church Council in 1655 approved the first revised book of prayer. Eastern prelates attended the council to ease their fears of heresy-contagion due to Moscow neglect. Uproar over how to make the sign of the cross required the verdict of a Church Council in 1656.

Nevertheless, dissent persisted in Kazan cathedral in Moscow. Ivan Neronov, a high priest, led the revolt, as did his colleague Avvakum, an ignorant fanatic, sent to Siberia and later burnt at the stake. The fierce persecutions continued in the wake of still another Church Council, which Nikon keynoted. Bishop Paul Kolomensky was removed from Moscow, as unanimity and obedience became all-important values.

The tsar had second thoughts about the wisdom of Nikon, and the two were estranged from 1658–66. Boyars were reputedly jealous of Nikon's influence and spread harmful tales about him. Finally, convinced that Nikon was "a peasant and stupid fellow," the tsar in December 1666 had Nikon deposed and removed to a monastery. Defiant, Nikon attacked as "tramps" the Moscow-subsidized Greek clerics he had recruited. Significantly, the 1666 Church Council delineated State and Church leading functions: the tsar alone would decide state affairs, and the patriarch be predominant inside the Church.

Nikonism without Nikon became the new reality. Reformist steps were sanctioned anew. The upper classes fell in line, and Old Believer sects had mostly independent peasants, Cossacks and merchants as adherents. An Old Believer hermit was found in 1978 in the forests of southern Siberia.

Historians were left to wonder over the rapid spread of the Great Schism. Many guessed it was a product of widespread social unrest. Unchallenged was an estimate that, from 1672 to 1691, almost 40 Old Believer mass suicides occurred and over 20,000 died from self-immolation.

Russian political culture would long bear an imprint of the dark features of Nikon's campaign. The infighting was highlighted by malicious rumormongering, denunciations and suspicion of papal plotting to undermine Orthodoxy. The voices were to be magnified in future periods of strain.

On the direct personal level, religion in Russia imparted calm and stoicism at moments of human emergency. In July 1914, Interior Minister N.A. Maklakov had to sign an army mobilization decree virtually equal to the opening of hostilities with Germany. He sat at a table laden with icons and ritual lamps. Maklakov spoke of impending revolution and crossed himself. “We cannot,” he said, “escape our fate.” After tremendous losses on a battleground of World War I, Russian soldiers sang the Easter hymn with the words “Christ is risen from the dead, conquering death by death.” An English listener wondered whether this was not the only weapon the men had to fight with.

Chapter III

The 'Westerners' Peter and Catherine

Empire and Vanity

Summary

The reign of Peter I (1682–1725) experienced only one year free of war. A larger than life figure, Peter strove for Russia to become a great power in Europe. That goal was reached when the modernized Russian Army defeated mighty Sweden. The Baltic coastline fell under Russian control. St. Petersburg, a new city, was built at huge human cost as gateway to northern shores and capital.

Internal reforms were decreed to remodel Russian society along Western lines – from dress to government structure. The Church resisted and was largely broken. Awed by victories and dynamic emperor, outsiders called Peter "The Real One."

Empress Catherine II (1762–96) was a brilliant and tireless self-promoter. Her policy agenda was on two tracks. First, she had to solidify and legitimize power, seized in a palace revolution. Hard line measures were basic ingredients of this process. The prestige of Russia and monarch soared with extension of the empire into Crimea and Poland. Second, Catherine promoted cultural activities, but her actions were more that of a Realpolitker than humanist.

***

Peter I was born in 1672 and reigned from 1682–1725. When aged 10, a half-sister, Sophia, was proclaimed regent, with Peter and brother Ivan V joint tsars. Sophia and her chancellor fell in 1694, and, five years later, Ivan died, and Peter headed the government. When Peter headed the government, a nation of 8 million and Moscow nobility of 10,000 were in law at his command. One of Peter's learned advisers felt compelled to espouse a doctrine of royal absolutism borrowed from the English theorist Thomas Hobbes.

Peter's temperament was shaped in a climate of palace intrigues and violence. As a child, he watched the heads of family supporters lifted on the pikes of disloyal soldiery. Some have traced to these shocks a nervous condition inciting compulsive movements of the head and face. Reflection and piety were never associated with this energetic figure. His life-long pleasures were hard drinking, playing the drum, and preparing fireworks.

In state business, military affairs preoccupied Peter. As a youth, he organized a juvenile army troop and imported European officers to train it. His first major campaign aimed at capturing Azov on the Black Sea from the Turks. The assault initially failed and required the building of 30 ships and 1,000 river barges for Russian troops to capture the port city.

At this time, the army was still a collection of ragtag militias. None could imagine that it would grow until, in 1721, it deployed 210,000 regulars and 100,000 Cossacks. A new sea-going navy would have 48 warships and 30,000 sailors.

Before Peter, the only port at Arkhangel served the Moscow state for trading with Western Europe. St. Petersburg was founded in 1703 to become the doorway for northern trade. Seven Baltic ports – including Riga in today's Latvia – were won in the Great Northern War against Sweden (1700–21). Wars with Turkey and Persia were less profitable. The cost of Petrine wars in life and limb was huge: one-fifth of village households disappeared or fled to distant areas.

Resentful of Peter's conquests, Austria and Britain withheld recognition of the new Russian Empire until after his death. Kliuchevsky believed that Peter distrusted the West and expected it to be scornful and unfriendly. The suspicion was gained no doubt from contacts with European bigwigs during the Russian ruler's travels to Europe. He visited Prussia, Holland, and England. At receptions, he was seen as coarse and unruly. Peter's powers of observation were acute and enabled him to learn manual crafts and detect the attitudes of hosts. The rumor mill too could have transmitted a sense of inferiority to generations of Muscovites.

Peter spared no effort to overtake the Europeans in every respect. The conservative nationalists were proud of their beards and caftans like those common in biblical times. The forced shaving of beards drew protests to the effect that victims were degraded to the unholy status of dogs, cats, and monkeys. Churchmen debated if such novelties might disrupt the salvation of souls. The merchants selling robes were flogged, sentenced to hard labor and their property confiscated. A revolutionary change for the faithful was an edict providing that the Church calendar would change from 1208, the alleged origin of the world, to 1689. The Patriarchate was later suspended, and a state board, the Holy Synod, replaced it as the highest body in the Russian church.

The central state bureaucracy was to play a leading role in reconstruction for empire- building. Central offices were created to control regions like Little Russia or Ukraine. The chiefs were sent to towns in 11 provinces to mobilize resources. Strongmen were named to run provinces. Old departments in the capital were turned into 15 Swedish-type "colleges." Bureaus expanded the state regulation of industry. Perhaps 200 factories were organized, albeit some resembled prisons. Expeditions were sent to map areas where minerals might be located and found rich deposits of iron ore and copper.

Peter acted to counter official misconduct. A sentence of death by hanging was imposed on Prince Gagarin, who ran and looted a Siberian province. The lesser punishment of flogging was meted out to the vice governor of St. Petersburg, two Senators and two princes. A major offender was Price Alexander Menshikov, who led a gang of thieves, but survived as a close adviser of the monarch. Peter was advised to curb his temper over stolen funds: "Is it possible for your Majesty to be emperor alone, without subjects? We all steal, only some do so more than others." The tsar is said to have feared that the state would collapse if corruption persisted.

A major defect of planned reform was the shortage of men qualified to fill new posts. Until Peter, the Moscow rulers had dreaded literacy as apt to introduce Western church heresies. Peter initiated secular education in Russia. Only 2,000 literacy schools to master the three R's were created, and most pupils were from military families. The nobility and gentry still resisted compulsory schooling for their children, who accounted for no more than 25 percent of those in literacy schools. Admiralty and war department schools taught mathematics and navigation to nobles. Peter laid the groundwork for a university at a new Academy of Sciences: It was generations before the needs of administration were met. Peter recruited many Germans and Scots for state service. Candidates for advanced learning were sent to study centers abroad. While these first steps to learn Western technique and thought were taken, muddle held sway in government. Admiral Count Fedor Apraksin wrote in a 1716 letter to Peter's aides: "Truly, we move about in all affairs as if we were blind and did not know what to do, there is a terrible state of confusion everywhere, and who will help us out and what shall we do next?"

Resistance to the Petrine reforms was largely silent. Even so, the army and security police had their hands full. Protests broke out against war and higher taxes to pay for it. New imposts on bathhouses and coffins were irksome. Religious dissenters had their income taxes doubled. Revolts broke out in Astrakhan (1705–06), Bashkiria (1705–11), and Don River Cossackdom (1707–08). Army deserters joined criminal gangs or fled to remote areas. An internal passport system to limit migration was decreed. The Secret Department in St. Petersburg reported on seditious talk that Peter "has become a Yid" (ozhidovilsia) and "The sooner Peter dies, the sooner military service will disappear, and things will get better for ordinary folk."

The family dramas of Peter were hidden from society. He first married at age 16 and broke the relationship two months later. Second wife, Marie Hamilton, was found guilty of killing an illegitimate child and executed. A son was accused of plotting and condemned to death. A third wife, the future tsarina Catherine I, was an illiterate peasant and long-time consort. She bore Peter II children, few of whom lived beyond infancy. The moody emperor found contentment in this plain person who accompanied him on military campaigns.

The "revolution from above" that Peter launched was recognized as such in Imperial history writing. Russia was moving somewhat closer to the standards of Western civilization. The cruelties were still many, and Russian scholars later regretted that European rulers had far earlier curbed thuggery among nobles. But the Petrine methods of governance were recognized as in keeping with the tsar's character, social conditions, and national habits.

It is hard to believe that Peter the Great sketched the guidelines of the Soviet crash program of military industrialization enacted two centuries later. Yet, the colorful tsar and dull "boss" Stalin were like partners in one mad dance. Both leaders were in a hurry to achieve Great Power status for Russia by raising war potential. Each brutally resorted to the use of forced labor on a huge scale for State projects. They were determined to break the Russian habits of apathy, inertness, and passivity. Peter faced more resistance: four large-scale revolts and three or four conspiracies. Stalin imagined the plotting and he purged elites. Imperial and Western historians termed the rush to industrialism of Peter and Stalin "revolution from above." A Maoist version of his model, "Great Leap Forward," was a failure.

Almost 40 years and six monarchs separate the reigns of Peter I and Catherine II.

Russian Tsars and Tsarevnas after Peter the Great:

Catherine I	1725–27
Peter II	1727–30
Anna	1730–40
Ivan VI	1740–41
Elizabeth	1741–62
Peter III	1762
Catherine II, the Great	1762–96

Peter's bloodline ended, and his dynastic marriages with Germans tangled the order of succession. Grouplets of insiders and officers of elite army regiments decided who should be enthroned. A whiff of constitutionalism mingled with palace conspiracies, state terrorism, serf unrest, and foreign wars. Russia became for some a European power during the international conflicts, but to some it was like Turkey or China until the 1850s.

As seen from our Table, Anna, a German, was the first post-Petrine ruler to keep the throne for more than two or three years. She was elected by a six-member Supreme

Secret Council whose kingpins came from the oldest aristocratic families. They imposed on Anna a number of Conditions. The Council would control Guards regiments or privileged units of the regular army that were led by noblemen. Draft laws of the Council would expand that body with elections involving the entire nobility. The privileges of nobles were to be enlarged, and their state service shortened. Schools for nobles were to become more numerous.

The new tsarevna and her faction were determined to scrap the Conditions and restore autocracy. Anna boycotted the Council sessions and named a new commander of Guards regiments. Afraid of Russian elites, Anna filled senior posts with trusted German expatriates.

In fact, a systemic persecution of Russian grandees occurred. The Baltic German Biron, an amoral and ignorant figure, gave his name to this period. The German Osterman led a disorderly state bureaucracy. A regiment of Baltic Germans was formed, and compatriot army generals appointed. Quite Russian was denunciation of subversives and the rise of pretenders who claimed to be sons of Peter the Great.

When Anna died, guardsmen seized Biron and a special court sentenced him to death; the verdict was changed to Siberian exile. Within a year, the child emperor, Ivan VI, and his mother, the regent, were deposed. Elizabeth, daughter of Peter the Great, was enthroned in a military coup.

A Russian resurgence was swift. The new "Little Mother" (matushka) Elizabeth is variably assessed in the works of Russian historians. S. M. Solovev extolled her for eliminating the German regime, calming national life, and acting humanely. Sergei Plantonov scoffed that Elizabeth was too Russian or addicted to having a good time. The negatives of Elizabeth are reckoned as powerful favorites; program-less government; and non-involvement of the sovereign in policy execution.

Under Elizabeth, the nobles gained more property rights and authority over the serfs. Only the long-term service duties of the nobility were unchanged. The aristocrats could only dream of exemption from state service.

Education grew into an upper class demand, and the Crown was accommodating. In 1755, Moscow University was opened – 550 years after the University of Paris. Ten professors were recruited for three departments: Law, Medicine, and Philosophy. A pair of high schools was attached, one for nobles and another for mixed social classes (raznochintsy). Rebels would later arise from the mixed-pupil schoolrooms.

The peasants lost meager rights to their overlords. In the years 1719–27, an estimated 200,000 serfs fled estates. Refuge was sought in South Russia, Urals, Siberia, and Poland. In the 1740s and 50s, serf revolts broke out as protest against cruelties. A 1760 edict allowed landowners to exile delinquent serfs to Siberia. The masters also had to approve of serfs assuming monetary obligations. The upper caste was still empowered as policemen and tax collectors. (The tax-paying male subjects in 1743 numbered 6.6 million and 7.3 million in 1761.) A clue to the low ethical standards of officialdom was an Imperial decree of 1760 rebuking law courts and government bureaus as "internal enemies" for their malfeasance.

One of the briefest reigns was that of the German Peter III. He arrived from German lands in 1762 and the same year was murdered. He is credited with freeing the nobility and gentry from state service. Otherwise, this royal eccentric was a hater of Russia and its customs. He closed the private chapels of wealthy subjects, ordered the clergy to destroy icons in churches and restricted Church property. Peasant revolts were registered, and whispers spread that Guards regiments were to be dissolved.

Hostility between Peter III and his magnetic German wife, Catherine, was capped at a state dinner. The tsar cursed his spouse and threatened her with arrest. Insiders knew and kept silent about a plot to dethrone Peter III. Catherine took command of guardsmen and household cavalry and was blessed as empress at the Kazan Cathedral in Moscow.

Russian foreign policy during this chaotic era focused on the quest for a balance of power in Europe. The five wars of Russia from 1725–62 have been viewed as too dynastic, expansionist, or acts of self-defense. One conflict was over royal succession in Poland; others were fought over land in Turkey needed to resist attacks and fear of Prussia. The financial and human costs of the wars were huge. But patriotism and pride rose in the higher echelons. Russian historians, like Nikolai Karamzin, glorified the Russian combatants.

Catherine II was born a princess in 1729 in a small German princedom. She was educated on French language texts and, at age 15, went to Russia to marry its crown prince. Catherine had to convert to the Orthodox Church, which Catherine I had called a great oak with roots deep in the ground. Catherine became an avid reader and wrote her collected works, which filled 12 volumes. The writings were meant largely for entertainment: children's stories, teachers' instructions, political pamphlets, history, dramatic plays, operettas and satirical songs, and a correspondence with European intellectuals.

Catherine did listen to Russian statesmen. Foreign Minister Count Nikita Panin convinced her that domination over Poland was essential for Russian safety and involvement in European affairs. Under the pretext of defending Orthodox Russian "dissenters" in Poland, Catherine sent over 15,000 troops into that fractured country. Russia joined with Prussia and Austria in three partitions of Poland (1772–93). The Russians were to be castigated in Western Europe during 1831and 1863 for their suppression of Polish revolts.

On the southern flank, Russia annexed Crimea in 1792, defeating Turkish forces, and advanced to the northern shore of the Black Sea. A Russian diplomat in Constantinople agitated for Catherine to stand up for Christians suffering under Turkish rule in the Balkan Peninsula. That was done, and new principalities there evolved into the state of Rumania. Constantinople seemed earmarked for Russian conquest.

Six wars made Catherine's reign one of the bloodiest in Russian history, and 200,000 square miles were added to the Russian empire. Old strategists of Catherine's foreign policy told young diplomats that, in the past, not a cannon was fired anywhere in Europe without an eye turned to the probable effect on Russia.

A 1783 census gave an overview of social interests. The population was reported at 32 million – 95 percent rural and 3 percent urban. Over half the peasants on gentry land were serfs, and 2.4 percent of subjects were "privileged." The clergy and merchants, each, were one percent of society. In Western Europe, towns were far more numerous at an earlier stage of development. The growth of an urban-based money economy there led to legal codes in the 11th century. By the 13th century, an English jurist could affirm that in his country law ruled – and not will. Until Catherine II, Russian monarchs were ill at ease with the idea of legal procedures that might reduce their authority. She made public gestures to dispel the belief that the government was a conspiracy against the nation. But her inspection tours of the provinces and easing the tax burden were insufficient to raise popular morale. The justice system had to be reformed.

Catherine wrote an Instruction for an assembly called the Legislative Commission. The 564 delegates were elected in 1767 and mostly officials, nobility and merchants. No serfs or local clerics were delegates. The throne's guidelines were for decentralization and a kinder, gentler version of absolute monarchy. Nobles and merchants were more interested in which class was worthier of owning serfs. The meetings were inconclusive. The gentry stayed firmly in the saddle.

Catherine was ambivalent; banning the use of torture in the questioning of suspected criminals and approving the punishment of peasants who complained about landlords. Public whipping and branding continued. Catherine awarded thousands of State peasants to favorites who wanted unpaid workers to toil on their estates.

A debate raged in the educated strata over how far tsarist Russia should go in adopting European values and institutions. One issue was to keep the use of violence in dealing with peasants suspected of criminal acts. An argument for toughness was made at a legal conclave in 1767: "Some people, when they do not see murder punished by torture and execution commit crimes more freely, peasants murder their lords; for this reason, cruel outrages, robberies, plunderings, and larceny of this type seem to be on the increase." Intellectual opponents advocated freedom for the serfs.

The prospect of serfdom reform faded with a large revolt of serfs, nomadic tribes and escaped convicts that broke out in 1773. A Cossack, Emelian Pugachov, led the rising under the pretense that he was the real tsar Peter III. The insurgents may have numbered 30,000, and 3,000 loyalists were slain before troops restored order.

The local administrations were revised in the wake of failure to avert the recent convulsion. New districts were put under "police captains," and "commandants" named to head towns. The nobility in 1785 was freed of corporal punishment; allowed to petition official acts; and made eligible for more judicial posts. The aristocrats remained a pillar of autocracy until 1917.

On balance, Catherine took a few steps forward. Public health became a state concern. The intellectual horizons of a few were broadened in lively journals. A Free Economic Society in St. Petersburg bestowed a prize on a scholar advocating the abolition of serfdom. Catherine, in 1771, granted to Old Believers a strip of land outside Moscow, and they kept a church there into the post-Soviet era. Public health did become a state concern. A Medical Commission required towns to provide physicians for entire districts, organize hospitals, and care for the disabled and mentally ill. Doctors were hired abroad, and local training courses started. Surgical instruments were to be produced and pharmacies organized. Slowly, Western ideas penetrated Russia and spread through philosophical clubs. Private presses existed, and 9,500 books were published during the 18th century. As self-styled "First landlord of Russia," Catherine kept silent about the evil of serfdom. But she may have hoped for eventual abolition. A liberal was chosen to be tutor of her grandson, the future tsar Alexander I.

Chapter IV

Rebels, Reformers, Diehards

Tsardom Beleaguered

Summary

The Romanov dynasty in 1913 celebrated its 300th anniversary. Governing elites were on edge as signs were cropping up of danger to the status quo at home and in Europe.

Until the abolition of serfdom in 1861, forced peasant labor was the core issue roiling society. Dissidents arose in the army officer corps and split into revolutionary- despotic and revolutionary-democratic wings. The "Decembrist" rising was crushed in 1825.

The land settlement reached after serfdom failed to satisfy the peasantry. Student agitators tried to provoke a rural upheaval and failed. A legal reform (in 1864) seemed to break ground toward constitutionalism. But the tsar was unresponsive to discontent over censorship, secrecy in government and absence of civil liberties. A terrorist assassinated Tsar Alexander II, serf-liberator, in 1881.

After a lull, several political parties were formed to represent the interests of peasants, workers, and professionals. The 1905 Revolution was a flash point and grand rehearsal for 1917. It climaxed in the granting of a weak parliament enfeebled still further thanks to a state coup restricting the voter lists.

In 1913, Panslavism drove Russian foreign policy. It was essentially an anti-German and anti-Austrian doctrine that worked on behalf of aggressive Slavic Serbia on the explosive Balkans Peninsula.

***

Russian officers were exposed to liberal ideas while serving in Europe during the Napoleonic Wars of 1813–14. They sent home entire libraries, started discussion clubs, and Masonic Lodges. Colonel Alexander Muravev founded in St. Petersburg an officers' society. General Mikhail Orlov did so in the provinces.

Colonel Paul Pestel joined Muravev's circle to promote constitutional government. They called themselves "Union or Salvation," stressing hierarchy and conspiracy. At the top were to be "boyars," and below "brothers," sworn to blind obedience. A body of "friends" or sympathizers was held in reserve. French and Italian secret societies were the model.

Mikhail Muravev decried such groups as criminal gangs, even though the goals were humanistic, and police spies were known to inform authorities of free thinkers. Ignoring skeptics, Pestel wrote a manifesto, "Russian Justice." It set as tasks the overthrow of the tsar, destruction of the royal family, empowering five men to suppress counter-revolution, electing a national assembly, outlawing non-Russian languages, abolishing Muslim discrimination of women and resettling Jews in Palestine. The Pestel agenda was for private land ownership, as well as communal and state properties. A Southern Society approved this revolutionary despotic charter.

In contrast, a Northern Society adopted a liberalizing plan drafted by a third Muravev, Nikita. A constitutional monarchy would feature a national legislature with rights to declare war, make peace, and grant amnesties. Provinces would get autonomy and each have an elected parliament (duma). Nikita wanted to free serfs, give the freedmen some land, but keep most acreage in private hands.

In December 1825, the insurgent officers tried to exploit confusion over royal succession and seize state power. They were outnumbered and disarmed. Tsar Nicholas I ordered the arrest of hundreds; 120 of 500 "Decembrists" were put on trial. Five were sentenced to death, and over 100 banished to Siberia.

The French ambassador was appalled at palace brutality and wrote a caustic assessment of Russian conditions: "The primary misfortune is that most intelligent people, those who were horrified and disgusted by the events [of December 14, 1825], think and say that reforms are essential, that a code of laws is needed; the justice system must be completely revamped; the peasants must be protected against the intolerable willfulness of the landowners. Rigidity is dangerous, and it is essential, even if later, to move with the times and immediately prepare decisive changes."

Nicholas I was determined to prolong the tightening up. In 1835, over 275 serf-owners or their bailiffs were killed. The military suppressed over half the 556 peasant disorders recorded under Nicholas. The most serious outbreaks were during the Crimean War in 1854. An imperial Manifesto ordered creation of a state militia to back up the regular army. A rumor swirled that serf volunteers would earn freedom and land. The rumor was officially denied, and peasants rioted in several provinces. Troops were needed to restore order. The spirit of reaction was assertive in foreign policy, too. The Russian army stifled a liberal revolt in Hungary, and alliances were struck with right wing Austria and Prussia.

The controversy between Westeners and inwards-looking Slavophiles intensified in the 1800s amidst an industrial boom. Peter Chaadaev told smug patriots to learn from the European model of civil development. Visarion Belinsky denounced serfdom, autocracy and the Orthodox Church, as well as corrupt officialdom.

Slavophils like Ivan Aksakov fired broadsides at the liberal press and intelligentsia, which craved for Europe's "constitutional rags." Western lawmakers were portrayed as bought in raw power struggles. The Russian peasantry was said to merit genuine self-rule to guard autocracy as a sacred virtue.

Panslavism was an offshoot of the Slavophil trend. Nikolai Danilevsky wrote the teaching manual Russia and Europe (1869). It traced to the West sources of Russian evils such as private property urges in villages. To ensure internal stability the communal form of land ownership was regarded essential as guarantee of equality.

Panslavism had implications for great power relations involving the Balkans Penninsula. The Russian government into the 1870s supported a fight for the independence of Slavic Bulgarian vassals of Turkey. Germanic Austria opposed national self-determination for rightless Slav nationalities in the Balkans. Panslavs exhorted racial brothers in East Europe to rise against the Germao-Roman world. Ultimately, Panslavs would campaign for Russian annexation of Constantinople as a strategic asset.

The socialism of European intellectuals became a beacon of humanism and class harmony for Russian political thinkers. "Utopian" Socialists imagined that Russia might avoid the painful stage of capitalist development. The peasant communes and co-operative associations would open a door to universal sharing of wealth. "Scientific" Socialists or Marxists, averred that Russia had to experience capitalism to learn culture.

Alexander Herzen (1812–70) sided with the Utopians in his younger years. He was born a rich nobleman and grew up adoring the Decembrists. A student radical, Herzen was banished to the provinces. He returned to Moscow and left for London for good. His Russian Free Press advocated liberty and social change in pamphlets and a journal smuggled into Russia. Disillusioned in old age, Herzen again fell under the spell of Russian civilization. Overall, he was the most respected of his nation's freedom activists.

George Plekhanov (1856–1918) was the leading Scientific Socialist or Marxist. In 1883, he organized a Liberation of Labor Group while in Swiss exile. He fought less ambitious colleagues who wanted more attention to economics than political pamphlet writing. Plekhanov deplored ruthlessness among the anti-monarchists.

Russia's defeat in the Crimean War by Britain and France convinced Tsar Alexander II (1855–81) that his realm was weaker and poorer than the first-class powers. He was also keen on stopping the revolts in the countryside. Alexander remarked in a speech to nobles in March 1856: "It is better to begin to destroy serfdom from above than to await the time when it begins to be destroyed from below." The audience was told to work out the details of emancipation.

The government and landlords reached a compromise in 1861. On average, the 20 million commune-based freemen got six acres of land each. The total amounted to one-half of the arable. The former serfs and their heirs had to pay for state bonds given to landlords over the next 50 years.

These redemption payments would be cancelled after the 1905 Revolution. In addition, freemen had to pay taxes, and, until the 1917 Revolution, complained of acute land shortage (malozemele). Yet, the peasantry ultimately owned more land than their one-time masters. The gentry lost a third of their income in the reform.

In the meantime, peasants rioted over debt in labor or rent to the estate owners. The military was sent to Bezdna village in Penza province; 55 were killed and 70 wounded. Elsewhere, mass floggings were carried out. Students held a vigil for Bezdna victims in the town of Kazan and the tsar ordered monks at the memorial exiled to a remote monastery.

A new wave of unrest swept over educated Russia. Writer Ivan Turgenev coined the term "Nihilists" to describe young iconoclasts in his novel Fathers and Sons. Brazen appeals to the young generation demanded abolition of police and revolt with axe and fire to kill monarchists. The son of a general was exiled to Siberia for inciting to insurrection. A turning point was a huge fire in Moscow blamed on Polish agents. The regime regained self-confidence when patriots rallied to support the suppression of a revolt of the hated Poles in 1863.

The law and local government reforms enacted in 1864 aimed at reconciling liberals and traditionalists. Juries were to decide criminal cases, and defense attorneys granted the right of appeal. The punishments would be less severe, and the public allowed in courtrooms. In time, some terrorist suspects were acquitted, and the Jewish defendant in a sensational murder trial was found innocent but hounded out of the country. Councils (zemstva) to promote education, public health, and farm skills were introduced under Marshals of the Nobility. The 1905 Revolution threw a scare into landowners, and they huddled in a hardline "United Nobility."

The young Nihilists viewed reforms from above as symptoms of weakness. One fired a pistol at Alexander II and missed. A campaign of "Going to the People" was launched in 1873 to foment peasant revolts. The crusaders were wrong to suppose that most villagers were communists by instinct and tradition. Betrayals to the police and mass trials followed.

A new conspiratorial grouplet, "Land and Liberty," was formed in 1876. Its terrorist section avenged police brutalities and specialized in bomb throwing. Victims included two chiefs of the security police and governor-general of Kharkov in Ukraine.

Ideologists of terrorism kept faith with the revolutionary-despotic school of the early 1800s. Europe was soon to learn of Mikhail Bakunin (1818–72), Sergei Nechaev (1847–83), and Peter Tkachev (1844–86). Their road to Socialism or statelessness was a quick coup of ruthless plotters. Simple Russians, they assumed, would exult if they prevailed.

The tsar-liberator, Alexander II, was mortally wounded in March 1881. A bomb was thrown and mutilated him on a street in St. Petersburg.

A leadership meeting was held at the Winter Palace to set the tone for the new reign. On one side were reactionaries: Holy Synod Chief K. P. Pobedonostsev, Education Minister DA, Tolstoy, and palace official Count S. G. Stroganov. The liberals at this special conference were State (Consultative) Council Chairman Grand Duke Konstantin Nikolaevich, Finance Minister A. A. Abaza, and War Minister D. A. Miliutin. Vacillators were Justice Minister A. N. Nabokov and Chairman of the Council of Ministers Count P. A. Valuev. Tsar Alexander Ill listened to the contending sides and cited warnings from the German emperor and Danish officials about the dangers of constitutionalism.

The meeting adjourned without a consensus on policy guidelines. Rumor had it that the peasants feared a return to serfdom. Alexander paid attention to right-wing journalists and told Pobedonostsev to write a Manifesto in defense of absolutism. Reformist insiders resigned their posts. New desks in the higher bureaucracy were given to men like Pazukhin, Marshal of the Nobility in Simbirsk province. His credentials were a newspaper article savaging the intellectuals.

Pobedonostsev is best remembered in the annals of Russian autocracy. Historian Pares describes him as "a jurist of first-rate ability and of absolute integrity, who, after taking a useful part in the great law reform of 1864, had become more and more reactionary as the revolutionary movement developed. Pobedonostsev was a firm believer in the old patriarchal Russia of Tsar, church and people, undisturbed by any perplexing modern ideas or developments. He pointed to perversions of the modern European press with the simple implication that absolute silence was better. He pointed to the manipulations of modern parliamentary life with the implication that the principle of national representation was essentially evil."

A polar opposite of this right-winger was the brilliant left-radical Vladimir llyich Ulianov (Lenin) born in 1870. This little attorney and Jules Martov (Tsederbaum) created in the capital the Fighting Union for liberation of the Working Class. In 1903, Lenin headed the Bolshevik, and Martov the Menshevik wing, of the Russian Social-Democratic Labor Party. Martov was a Europe-type moderate, while Lenin was a throwback to the age of Colonel Pestel. Menshevik Leon Trotsky (Bronshtein) in 1904 sketched Lenin's tyrannical style of leadership: "The party must substitute itself for the working class; then the party caucus for the party, then the Central Committee for the caucus; and finally, a dictator substitutes himself for the Central Committee."

By then, the peasant-based Social-Revolutionary Party was in the vanguard of progressive movements. Peasant grievances were listed in a memo that Finance Minister Witte sent to Tsar Nicholas II in 1898: corporal punishment, willful taxation, restricted movement, and absence of inheritance laws. Agrarian reformers created the Social-Revolutionary (SR) Party in 1900. Socialization of land and a federal state were keystones of SR belief. A Combat Detachment was dedicated to terrorism, and assassinated Education Ministers Sipiagin (1902) and Plehve (1904) and Grand Duke Serge, governor-general of Moscow (1905). The SR Evno Azev was a police agent exposed in 1908 and served to discredit the regime abroad.

Eventually, the big property-owners, industrialists, and intellectuals who were monarchists formed their own parties. The Constitutional, Democratic, and "Octobrist" parties looked to West Europe for a political model. Russian nationalism and imperialism were strongly felt in this crowd.

The 1905 Revolution broke suddenly over the Russian political scene. January 22nd was "Bloody Sunday," a massacre of workers who were demonstrating in the capital to protest neglect of basic needs. Strikes and strike committees or soviets were organized until 3 million workers laid down their tools. The crew of the battleship Potemkin mutinied and sailed the vessel to Rumania. Defeats in a war with Japan angered the public. Zemstva called for a national assembly and genuine trade unions, unlike police-run stooges.

The tsar was pressured to issue an October Manifesto granting civil liberties and establishing a feeble parliament, the State Duma. Tensions were defused, and the last armed rebels were subdued in Moscow at year's end.

A showdown of modernity versus monarchy developed in the spring 1906. The parliament Nicholas II conceded to break the 1905 Revolution opened. A broad electorate lent a liberal complexion to the gathering. Appeals were made for land grants for peasants by the compulsory expropriation of privately owned lands: home rule for national minorities; and abolition of privileges accruing by reason of class, ethnicity, religion, or sex. A general amnesty for political prisoners was on the liberal agenda.

The government rejected amnesty and upheld its decrees for emergency powers to stem rampant "murders, robberies and shocking acts of violence." Resettlement of land-hungry peasants in Siberia was favored over deputies' proposal on the peasant question.

The State Duma, as the parliament was called, voted no confidence in the government and accused it of "a clear unwillingness to avert new shocks and dislocations in our country." A few weeks later an imperial decree dissolved the Duma. Monarchism had won the duel with modernity and this would not change until 1917.

Diehards to the bone, Nicholas II and his stern wife were determined to neutralize the incipient constitutional form of government. In 1906, a new premier was named – energetic and tough Peter Stolypin, a former governor and Interior Minister, who cracked down on law-breakers. Stolypin had a pragmatic side, devising a plan for peasants to take as personal property their share of communal property. Respect for personal ownership was to be built in the volatile countryside.

In June 1907, Stolypin organized a state coup restricting voter lists for the State Duma. He wanted to extend the zemstva into western provinces. But high-level opposition irked Stolypin, who told a Russo-American journalist that "it is erroneous to think that the Russian cabinet – even in its contemporary united form – is a political power in its own right. It is only the reflection of such a power. You must understand the aggregate of pressures and influences which are constraints on the Government. In certain questions, there exist areas inaccessible to us. I can only maneuver." Stolypin was assassinated in 1911.

The pendulum swung back to reaction once police fired on strikers in the Lena River gold field in Siberia. Alexander Krivoshein, an influential grandee, rarely said in a 1913 speech that impeding social progress was a distinction between "us," the Government, and "them," the people.

Strikes rose in 1914, and this development has been appraised variously in American commentaries. Some view the labor actions as only signs of modernity; others detect a clue to imminent revolution. A number of provinces were then under a type of martial law, which favors the darker surmise.

Did the Russians sense a danger of war? Some German statesmen did. The Chancellor asserted early in 1914 that Russia had become a "colossus which threatens the civilization of Europe." In St. Petersburg, the million-man Russian army was thought to be a reliable counter-weight to the Prussian legions. The devastating power of modern weapons was unimaginable. Russia's infantry was touted as a "steamroller," compensating for the German output of 14 million tons of steel annually, as opposed to Russia's 4.1

million output. Allied with France to secure loans to finance industrialization, Russian leaders apparently were reassured enough to champion Panslavism, a doctrine challenging to Germany, which was allied to Austria-Hungary, an empire fearful of Serbia, Russia's aggressive Balkan client. The tsar should have put aside his game of dominoes and paid attention to a memo written in February 1914 by ex-Interior Minister P.N. Dumovo. He advised that the interests of Russia and Germany were nowhere in conflict. Ignorance, delusion, and pride went before a monumental fall.

Chapter V

World War and Revolution

Over the Edge

Summary

In July 1914, a European crisis arose. Russia aligned with France and Great Britain against Germany and Austria-Hungary. War came, and, three years later, the Russian army fragmented.

Since 1915, the home front was pulling in opposite directions. Zemstva cared for many wounded soldiers. Duma liberals pressed the Tsar to enact constitutional reforms. Nicholas was unmoved. The regime cracked down on Bolsheviks, who got German funding for their anti-war propaganda. Refugees flooded into the homeland from western provinces lost to the Germans, and this further strained basic facilities.

In 1916, the Duma heard a bitter speech condemning the Government's ineptitude. The murder of crooked palace favorite Rasputin failed to restore respect for the throne. Bread riots hit the capital. Nicholas had to abdicate, and a Provisional Government was formed. A military coup was foiled, and chaos prevailed. In November 1917, Lenin staged a coup, and the Bolsheviks seized State power. Russia was to become a platform for the launching of universal revolution.

***

A Bosnia Serb terrorist, Gavrilo Princip, on June 28, 1914, shot and killed the Austrian heir apparent Archduke Franz Ferdinand. The crime occurred in the Bosnian town of Sarajevo, located in a province annexed by Austria-Hungary in 1908 and, since, a lost territory in Serb eyes. The Vienna government had no proof that Serb officials plotted the Sarajevo outrage, but suspected it was the work of the influential Black Hand society in Serbia. A secret decision was reached to crush Serbia and partition it with neighboring states. Since then, historians have been trying to identify from documents and memoirs who really lit the fuse to the Balkans power-keg.

Those suspected of complicity number less than 12. The civil executives were:

Kaiser Wilhelm II	Germany
Emperor Franz Joseph	Austria-Hungary
Foreign Minister Leopold von Berchtold	Austria-Hungary
Tsar Nicholas II	Russia
Foreign Minister Sergei Sazonov	Russia
President Raymond Poincare	France
Foreign Secretary Sir Edward Grey	Great Britain

The military Chiefs of Staff who were central in the march to war:

Count Helmut von Moltke	Germany
Baron Conrad von Hötzendorf	Austria-Hungary
General N. N. Yanushkevich	Russia

Diplomatic historian A. J. P. Taylor thinks that Germany played a decisive role in bringing on World War I. The argument is that Wilhelm took all basic decisions and agreed, on July 5, 1914, with a letter from Franz Joseph saying that "Serbia must be eliminated as a political factor in the Balkans" and "friendly settlement is no longer to be thought of." This gave to Austria-Hungary a free hand or blank check to crush Serbia. The Kaiser did not believe that Russia, patron of Serbia, was ready for war, and he expected Britain and France to be neutral in a localized fight between Austria-Hungary and Serbia. Observers tend to accent the view that Austria-Hungary would never have moved against Serbia without Germany's assurance that it would deter Russia from war on behalf of Serbia.

Historian B. H. Sumner blames Austria-Hungary for being unwilling or unable to solve its nationalities problem. The Kaiser's envoy at Vienna had cabled Berlin in May 1914 that the Austro-Hungarian partner's state structure was "cracking at every joint." On the eve of the Sarajevo crime (June 24, 1914), Berchtold wrote a memorandum accusing Russia of trying to encircle Austria-Hungary and aiming at eventual hegemony in Europe. Vienna, like Berlin, underrated Russian will to keep Serbia as a barrier between Germany and the Turkish Straits- vital waterway for grain shipments to Western Europe. After all, the initiative for a showdown in the Balkans came from Vienna.

Berchtold addressed the Austro-Hungarian Council of Ministers on July 7 and said that Germany preferred to have a European war before Russian armaments were completed. Russia was claimed to seek a league of Balkan states in order to provoke them against Austria-Hungary when the moment seemed favorable.

When the tsar decided to confront Austria-Hungary and Germany, he was acclaimed by upper and middle classes. The workers stopped their strikes and turned patriotic. Peasants failed to recognize the enemy and rioted over call-ups during harvest time.

Luigi Albertini, who wrote three volumes on the origins of World War I, held Russian leaders most negligent in the run-up to war. He points out that, in January 1914, Prime Minister Goremykin was linked to Panslav nationalists in an anti-German faction. Foreign Minister Sazonov was powerless against this group, bonded by kinship with Serbia and intent on stopping the German drive into the Middle East through Constantinople.

Upon learning of an Austro-Hungarian ultimatum to Belgrade infringing on Serb national sovereignty, Sazonov decided on a firm response. On July 20, the tsar approved of partial mobilization, a step to humiliate the Austrians. The measure was unworkable and, on July 30, changed to full-scale war readiness. Germany equated this action to a state of war and insisted on a Russian back down. St. Petersburg refused, and, on August 1, Germany declared war on Russia. The Kaiser's envoy to Russia was tearful, as he met Sazonov and recognized the failure of his mission.

Historian Florinsky sees Germany, Austria-Hungary, and Russia wrong-headed about security goals. He contends that "concepts of national interest held by the leaders of the three Eastern empires were illusory and destructive of the cause they were supposed to secure." This appears to mean that Germany could not hope to establish a political dictatorship over Europe. Austria-Hungary had to remove Germanism as a pillar of rule. The Russians had to turn their backs on Panslavism and no longer view the Balkans as a back door to the Turkish Straits. All were unlikely prospects, and one can surmise from this analysis that World War I was inevitable. Was delay an option, if there is always choice?

Albertini is critical of Allied leaders Poincare and Grey. The French President visited St. Petersburg in early July 1914 and no doubt urged firmness in dealing with Berlin and Vienna. This risky stand contrasted with the inaction of the British Foreign Secretary during the crisis. Slow thinking is one anti-Grey criticism, another is that Englishmen are unable to penetrate into the psychology of other peoples. The astute Scot Seton-Watson vindicates Russian policymakers. He fails to see practical alternatives to Russian neutrality: "Abandon the Serbs" and "accept a status of permanent inferiority to the two German powers and raise serious doubts in the minds of the French whether she was worth having as an ally or she could go to war." Seton-Watson reminds about Russia that, "judged by the conventional wisdom of international diplomacy in 1914, her decision to go to war was fully justified." But did it appreciate disastrous Russian backwardness?

Tsar Nicholas' army of 1.4 million had few elite regiments and a limited supply of material. The leadership was no match for the German high command, which had studied poor Russian performance in the Russo-Japanese War. Seniority and connections were criteria of promotion to higher command. Nor was the Intelligence department adept.

In spite of failings, General Yanushkevich, on July 29, pressed Sazonov to bring total mobilization. He had the backing of commander-in-chief Grand Duke Nicholas and Quartermaster General Yuri Danilov. The tsar realized that his cousin, the Kaiser, was only pretending to act as a mediator in the crisis and sided with his warlords. Dictatorial authority was granted to commanders in undefined military zones, and they soon clashed with province governors over administrative issues

Austria-Hungary declared war on Serbia (July 28) and fired shells at Belgrade. Conrad's invading troops killed 5,000 civilians before meeting serious resistance. Austrian officers had instilled in troops the hateful view of Franz Ferdinand about Serbs – thieves and murderers. German occupiers in France and Belgium were ruthless; the tsar was asked to divert German divisions from the Western front. Paris was saved!

A Russian offensive into East Prussia was launched in August 1914. It cost 30,000 dead and 125,000 prisoners. A month later, the Turks bet on German victory and closed the Straits, the main Allied supply route to Russia. The tsarist army continued attacking and captured half of Galicia, a region between Poland and Ukraine that Austria-Hungary had controlled.

The occupation of Galicia was painful for 3 million Ukrainians and 350,000 Jews. Greek Orthodoxy was imposed on Christians by priests sent from Russia. Ukrainian intellectuals and clergy were deported to the east, as were Jews, whose Yiddish language sounded like German and aroused suspicion that they might be German agents. Over the next two years, 2 million refugees are estimated to have been wandering inside Russia. After more fighting and heavy losses, Grand Duke Nicholas, in December 1914, informed the Allies that his stocks of munitions were so low that his army had to stay on the defensive.

Alexander Helphand was a rich fellow traveler of the Bolsheviks and, in January 1915, met with the German Ambassador to Turkey. He advised the funding of Lenin, who, in Swiss exile, was agitating for the destruction of tsarism and division of Russia into small states. The German foreign office accepted the proposal to sponsor Lenin, whom they paid 200,000–250,000 marks or $50,000–$62,000 to conduct anti-war propaganda in Russia. Under his breath, Lenin probably scoffed at the German bureaucrats as "useful idiots."

In 1915, Lenin summoned the proletarians of Europe to revolt and end the Great War. Bolshevik members of the Duma were arrested and tried for subversive activity. Their fate was prison or Siberia. The military and bases in Russia appeared to be stable.

The calm was deceptive, and, from May to September 1915, the Germans advanced on the eastern front. Poland and Lithuania fell. Russian losses were over 300,000 dead and 1.5 million missing or prisoners. Mass surrenders and desertions were alarming. Krivoshein warned the Government that "The great migration [of refugees] organized by Headquarters leads Russia to the abyss, to revolution, to perdition."

That summer, the public was restive. Newspapers in Yaroslavl, a province of the central industrial region, noted high prices and a beef crisis that caused a dramatic rise of the consumption of horsemeat. Urban strikes resumed as real wages declined.

The growth of civil society groups strengthened Duma moderates. A zemstvo Red Cross won the respect of educated citizens, as did a War Industry Committee with worker sections that converted small factories to munitions output. Kadets and Octobrists, in September 1915, convened a "Progressive Bloc." It denounced the regime's distrust of public initiative. The Bloc demanded a government chosen by tsar and Duma, legality, restriction of military power in local affairs, limited amnesty of political offenders, Polish autonomy, repeal of anti-Semitic laws, lifting of bans on the Ukrainian press and the return of exiles, freedom of trade unions, equalization of peasants with other classes, and geographic expansion of zemstva. Premier Goremykin went to the tsar, who had recently become commander-in-chief, and was ordered to close the Duma. A two-day protest was called in Petrograd or renamed capital. Several liberalizing state ministers were dismissed.

The grimmest of forecasts was sent from Duma President Rodzianko to Premier Goremykin in January 1916: "A general disintegration in all branches of our national life, coupled with a lack of essential commodities, is growing in the rear of our national armies." The Duma was powerless and "cannot therefore be held responsible for the inevitable and imminent collapse."

The empress and her corrupt guru, Grigori Rasputin, raised to head of Government the shallow reactionary Boris Sturmer. British Ambassador George Buchanan wired London that Sturmer would remain in the Allied camp, but said he was a "man on whose word no reliance can be placed, and whose only idea is to further his own ambitious ends."

Under Sturmer, General A. A. Polivanov, War Minister and friend of Octobrist leader A. I. Guchkov, was removed in March 1916 for controlling too loosely the civil society groups in the industrial sector. The empress feared the groups as the nucleus of a new Government. Prince Georgi Lvov, chairman of the zemstvo Union to assist the war effort, would head the Provisional Government formed after the March 1917 revolution.

New supplies led Headquarters to think that one major offensive was possible, even if steel helmets and gas masks were lacking. General A. A. Brusilov, in September 1916, led an offensive against Austrian forces. The Russians took 375,000 prisoners before the drive was checked, and attackers suffered 550,000 casualties. Like Mary Todd Lincoln told the U.S. President in 1864 about federal General Grant, the hysterical tsarina wrote to Tsar Nicholas in October 1916: "Oh, give your order again to Brusilov to stop this useless slaughter."

The next month, Kadet leader Miliukov at the Duma implied that chaos was the result of governmental incompetence. The speech was copied and distributed to the public. A handful of aristocrats hoped to save the dynasty by eliminating the "evil genius" Rasputin and murdered him in December 1916. That was a futile gesture, and, a few weeks later, 300,000 demonstrators in Petrograd marked the anniversary of the Bloody Sunday massacre that sparked the 1905 Revolution.

An Allied conference was held in Petrograd in February 1917 to coordinate strategy and resources. Bread riots soon shook the capitol. The garrison mutinied, and mob rule prevailed. Policemen and army officers were killed, the main prison seized, and law courts burned. The tsar ordered suppression of the disorders, but front-line generals advised him to abdicate. He did so, and the throne was to be vacant until a constitution-making assembly decreed the best form of government. Some liberals were disturbed that a unifying factor was removed from the national scene.

To restore order at the center, Duma improvised a Provisional Government of liberals and moderate socialists. A parallel body to express worker and soldier opinion was the Soviet of 2,500 delegates led by SRs, Mensheviks, and Bolsheviks. The Soviet's initial ruling put the army on its last legs: Army Order Number One empowered military committees to control weapons and ensure discipline as well as hear soldier grievances.

Vernadsky explains the weakness of the Provisional Government: "Educated on the principles of European constitutionalism, they tried to apply these principles to the conditions of Russia without taking into account the revolutionary nature of that era. It required rapid decisions and not scrupulous observance of constitutional procedure." We must keep in mind, too, the vague belief of liberals that they had to sustain the war effort to ensure the goodwill of British and French statesmen, who, after victory over Germany, would help Russia navigate a difficult transition to democracy.

The Provisional Government issued a decree that resembled the program of the Duma Progressive Bloc. A new wrinkle was to keep revolutionary troops in the capital and forbid their departure for the front lines.

The Germans enabled Lenin to return to Russia on a special train that included other Russian emigres. Once at home, the Bolshevik leader campaigned for an immediate socialist revolution. Soldiers were told to fraternize with German and Austrian enemies. Until then, Bolsheviks in Russia were committed to a defensive war, and Lenin had to convince them to turn leftward – which he did.

In June 1917, new Premier Alexander Kerensky rejected the opinion of his generals and tested the alliance of Government and Army. He ordered army remnants to advance into Galicia.

The push failed, and a German counter-attack led to the panicky flight of the Russians. The estimates of Russian casualties from 1914 through 1917 are: 1.3–1.7 million dead, 2.5–4.2 million wounded and 2.4–3.6 million prisoners and missing. A Church and a military cemetery for the war dead were each built in Moscow. Bolsheviks in power destroyed both sites, leaving one grave intact.

While Kerensky was at the front, a demonstration of sailors and workers in Petrograd may have signified that a Bolshevik coup was underway. Cossacks and a surviving Guards regiment dispersed the demonstrators. Lenin fled into Finland, and army commander-in-chief General Lavr

Kornilov seemed about to lead a right-wing coup. That menace vanished in events pointing toward a coalition of Soviets and Bolsheviks.

An agrarian revolution occurred in the summer and autumn of 1917. Villagers seized the landed estates, and wealthy peasant farms were plundered. The traditional rural commune assemblies directed a "black repartition" of nobles' land that was the dream of the poorest farmers for centuries.

Still, another centrifugal force was the national minorities, who comprised almost half of the population and sought independence. The Petrograd Soviet approved of Polish statehood, and a Finnish national assembly did the same on behalf of its people. Nationalities and Cossacks sent 100 delegates to a congress held in September 1917. A reconstruction of Russia as a federation of sovereign states was envisaged. The Ukrainian Rada (Council) proclaimed independence, but that was short-lived (see below).

Lenin skillfully timed his seizure of power. The elections for a constitution-making assembly were set for November 25, 1917. Deputies were to meet December 12. A nationwide Congress of Soviets was due November 7. That night, Lenin's squads toppled the Provisional Government and the Soviet Congress cheered the Bolsheviks' peace-with-land platform.

The Bolshevik overthrow of Kerensky was managed by Trotsky, who set up a small group of workers and sailors to arrest the Cabinet at the Winter Palace. In charge was the flamboyant Antonov-Ovseyenko, who was to serve as Soviet envoy to Madrid in the Spanish Civil War and victimized in the Stalin purges. Stalin, as Commissar for

Nationalities in 1918, wrote for Pravda an article lauding Trotsky as organizer of Lenin's putsch. Stalin as dictator had aides lionize himself as the tactician of the 1917 Bolshevik overthrow.

Soviets quickly took power in the outlying towns, and commune assemblies ran the countryside. Many expected a Bolshevik demise in the ensuing few weeks. The appeal of Lenin's slogans was not appreciated. Decisively, the Bolsheviks banned the liberal press and created the secret police (Cheka or Extraordinary Commission) to silence critics. Abroad, idealists hailed a Lenin decision to publish wartime "secret treaties" that ceded to Russia Constantinople, Kurdistan, and Armenia. Nevertheless, enough domestic opponents of Bolshevism remained for a vicious civil conflict to be fought over the following three years.

In the 1920s and 30s, attention was drawn to Bolshevik winners and losers in 1917. The leaders were at odds from August to October. Lenin and Stalin faced-off against a cautious group of Grigori Zinoviev and Lev Kamenev. As a Central Committee member, Stalin keynoted a Bolshevik convention, with Lenin hiding in Finland. The chief was hunted by Russian police for involvement in July riots that looked like a Bolshevik coup. Stalin argued that Socialist revolution might occur first in Russia and not in Europe, as widely believed in radical circles. This was the logical prelude to Stalin's credo of "Socialism in One Country."

In October, Lenin fought Zinoviev and Kamenev, whom he disparaged as "strikebreakers" of revolution since they opposed an immediate Bolshevik coup. Zinoviev and Kamenev were fearful of anti-Bolshevik sentiment in the provinces. Lenin's "theses" were adopted by the inner circle and became a Party model of sage boldness.

Lenin, in November 1917, was impatient to realize the old Russian revolutionary dream of expunging feudal survivals. Stalin wished to earn the reputation of a Russia firster, deeply skeptical of internationalism, legality, and compromise. Inwardly, Stalin may not yet have been an Ivan IV-type monster but revealed loyalty to a markedly Eastern brand of politics. The third who made a revolution, flamboyant Trotsky, was quite a literary stylist and took special note of his own dramatic moments for posterity. What the Bolsheviks called the "heroic period" of the Russian Revolution soon unfolded.

Chapter VI

The Red Era

Bread but No Butter

Summary

The Soviet dictatorship navigated between real or imaginary foes during its relatively short history (1917–91). The six stages of Soviet evolution were:

1. War Communism. A moneyless-barter economy existed, the Red Terror was unleashed, and the Communist International was organized to foment world revolution.
2. The New Economic Policy made concessions to hard-pressed peasants and legalized small traders.
3. Stalin's farm collectivization and military industrialization programs were to overcome a 50 to 100-year lag of economic development. The Great Terror and westward expansion drove to 10 million the number of State victims since 1932.
4. War with Nazi Germany and the need to bolster morale required tolerance of the Orthodox Church

and a surge of Russian nationalism. Symbolically, the alliance with Britain and America evoked abolition of the Communist International.

5. Stalin's last moves were to shape an empire in East Europe, sanction war in Korea and order repressions in East Europe and inside the USSR.
6. Half-reforms were initiated after Stalin, and the more robust novelties of M. S. Gorbachev led to the collapse of the system.

***

A Congress of Soviets met on November 7, 1917, and sanctioned peace with Germany and land to peasants. Mensheviks and Social-Revolutionaries left the Congress in protest. Left SRs remained and received token representation in the Bolshevik government. The elections for a constitution-making assembly resulted in the SRs winning nearly three-fifths of the votes; the Bolsheviks got over one-quarter. Lenin argued that the election machinery was flawed and the vote invalid.

The Constituent Assembly met in January 1918, and Red sailor guards shut it down. A state based on constitutional law was ruled out for the duration of Soviet power. Lenin won an internal party debate over peace terms and made vast territorial concessions to Germany. The Allied victory in November 1918 saved the Soviets from long-term acceptance of the Treaty of Brest-Litovsk, which Lenin called "obscene."

Civil war erupted in late 1917 and lasted until 1921. It is estimated that 800,000 died in the conflict and 2 million emigrated. Homeless children (bezprizorniki) roamed city streets for years.

The national psyche was scarred in the latest fratricide. Chekists executed over 400 rebels on the heels of an anti-Soviet revolt in Yaroslavl in July 1918. Menshevik leader Martov was allowed to address the Soviet Congress in December 1919 and accused the Cheka of a "monstrous growth of terror." British expert John Maynard reckoned that, from 1917 to 1922, the Cheka shot 5,000 Orthodox priests and 28 bishops. White General Budberg, in a diary entry of May 3, 1919, thought it was harmful for his troops to "rape, flog, rob, torture, and kill indiscriminately and without restraint."

The forces of Allied intervention in the Russian civil war were small, except for the Japanese units in eastern Siberia. Bolshevik anti-Western propaganda was loud and lasting. The Soviet Russian republic constitution of 1918 saw the world divided into two hostile camps of capitalism and socialism. The Communist International (Comintern) founded in 1919 dedicated the Soviet regime to sponsor foreign radical groups aiming at the overthrow of Western governments. It would survive until 1943 and revived in 1947 as an Information Bureau committed to the two-camp doctrine.

Only as late as 1920, did White General Wrangel have the good sense to offer peasants a liberal policy. By then, the Red Army attained a superiority of 10 to 1. Tsarist officers were coerced or persuaded to lead the Red Army. A revolutionary war into newly freed Poland was unsuccessful in 1920, and some prized Ukrainian farmlands were lost until World War II. Most of Ukraine, however, fell to Soviet forces in 1919 and yielded wheat, coal and iron ore.

While fervent Bolsheviks canonized as heroic Lenin's anti-market policies of 1918–20 the illustrious Moscow historian Yuri Got'e had bitter thoughts about the national character. He wrote in a 1919 diary entry: "To tell the truth, there was little honesty under the old [Tsarist] regime, which was entirely immersed in dishonesty, but this [Bolshevik] order, which is itself built on lies and deceit, is even more suitable for all sorts of villains and scoundrels…how profoundly right I was staying out of Russian political life, which besides intrigues and cliquishness there was – and always will be – nothing. All the parties are only masks for ambitious men and traps for fools; and ruling parties are in addition an instrument for scoundrels."

Russia was devastated in international and civil wars. By 1921, the population had shrunk from 172 million in 1914 to 132 million. Manufacturing was down to 13percent of 1913's output. The per capita national income dropped more than 60 percent.

Dictatorship was unpopular among anarchistic peasants, workers, and sailors. A bloody clash at the Kronstadt naval base pitted insurgents against Bolsheviks, who massacred defeated and wounded foes. Lenin offered an olive branch to farmers, who had suffered under civil war requisitioning. The 10th Congress of Bolsheviks in March 1921 approved a tax on farm surpluses to replace the forced product collections. Private trade and small business were legalized. The state would keep control of large-scale industries.

One-party rule was strengthened to restrain free marketers. A secret resolution of the 10th Congress banned "factionalism" or creating inner-party lobbies for promotion of special interests. Central Committee members who might try to influence opinion at the policymaking Politburo were to lose their high status. Old Bolshevik Miasnikov wrote a letter to Party leaders urging freedom of speech and press for all Russians "from the monarchists to the anarchists." When Lenin told Miasnikov not to state his views at Party meetings, he replied: "You have no faith in the working class…You believe in the clerks. That is your misfortune." Miasnikov was expelled from the Party.

Stalin was Commissar for Nationalities and head of the monitoring body Worker and Peasant Inspectorate. As Party General Secretary, Stalin was to enforce the ban on factionalism. He wove his own network of associates during the civil war, and they had since become Party, army and police officials.

Lenin wrote a testament describing Stalin as a bully who should be demoted. Trotsky seemed to be Lenin's choice for political heir. Stalin was able to stay in the saddle thanks to an odd turn of events: Lenin died, and his confidants assured Party workers that Stalin had mended his bad ways. Stalin posed as a Lenin disciple, faithful to the moderate New Economic Policy (NEP), while leftists decried mounting social inequality and absence of economic planning.

A challenge to Stalin was raised before the Party Congress in December 1925. Lenin's widow joined

Politburo members Zinoviev and Kamenev to indict Stalin for making concessions to private farmers and State executives.

Stalin privately read a theory article by Zinoviev and told an associate that he "decoded the double meanings" and learned that its author was attacking the General Secretary's partner Nikolai Bukharin, as a new Stolypin, the tsarist premier who championed peasant land-owning.

Zinoviev's worker base in Leningrad urged Moscow bosses to unite with them and oust Stalin for:

- concealing Soviet Russia's growth into a peasant kingdom;
- allowing the State machine to pressure the Kremlin and dictate policy;
- ignoring Leningrad and degrading it to the level of a simple province; and
- failing to see the mediocrity of Bukharin and Stalinist Viacheslav Molotov, as well as Stalin's lack of analytical capacity.

The Zinovievites effectively framed a power conflict as a class struggle, claiming "proletarian" Leningrad and "petty bourgeois" Moscow.

At the Party Congress, Stalin was attacked for making the Central Committee Secretariat a switchboard of power. The rebels were heavily out-voted, and pro-Stalin chants introduced. Kamenev was demoted, and Leningrad subdued.

Stalin, in June 1927, wrote a letter to security chief Menzhinsky ordering mass arrests of anti-Soviet elements.

Show trials and confessions of the accused in open courtrooms were proposed. The operation began with shooting of 20 former monarchists and the arrest of 9,000 farmers. Suddenly, the campaign of terror was halted.

The Trotskyites, in November 1927, joined a Moscow demonstration honoring the Bolshevik Revolution and carried anti-regime placards. Stalinist bands dispersed them, and Trotsky was exiled to Central Asia. Still insisting that the USSR was a workers' state, Trotsky was killed in 1940 by a Soviet agent in Mexico.

Settlement of the Lenin succession issue had a logical upshot. In December 1929, still another un-Marxian development burst onto the Soviet landscape: Stalin's cult of personality. His 50th birthday was celebrated although it was really 1878, not 1879, as falsely stated on a Party questionnaire. The Russified Georgian drew on the tradition of Russian folk heroes, such as Tolstoy's infallibly wise peasant Platon-Karataev.

NEP enabled a recovery of Russian production by 1926–28. A famine, however, loomed over towns, as private grain farmers threatened to strike over low prices for the purchase of their output. Stalin adopted in 1928–29 five-year industrial planning and collectivization of agriculture. The plans focused on a buildup of heavy industries as a growth stimulator and bedrock of military power. A series of local civil wars were fought in the countryside. Peasants slaughtered their livestock and ate the meat. A famine raged in 1932–33, and 5–7 million died. Industrial accidents were blamed on "wreckers," and engineers scapegoated at show trials. Stalin said a lag of 100 years behind the West had to be overcome in a decade.

Some Old Bolsheviks lost confidence in Stalin. To stir Party opinion, M. N. Riutin, a high official expelled in 1930 for oppositionist views, wrote and circulated an anti-Stalin manifesto. Riutin argued for reversal of basic policies and the ouster of Stalin. His picture of Stalin is remarkable: "crafty, ambitious and spiteful, treacherous and envious, hypocritical and insolent, boastful and stubborn." Riutin was arrested in 1932, sentenced to 10-years' imprisonment and shot in 1937.

In 1937–38, Stalin executed his decade-old terror plan. A slight improvement in urban living standards enabled Stalin to proclaim that life had become "better, more gay." One-time critics were prosecuted as traitors and made to confess to falsified evidence. The secret police recorded 350,000 executions in 1937, and 330,000 in 1938.

The most astounding press bulletin of the Great Terror surfaced on June 12, 1937. It said that the death sentence was carried out on eight Red Army generals. The deceased were charged with having engaged in military espionage for a foreign state. The German ambassador in Moscow reported a theory that "Stalin fears independent leaders in the army as possible food for dissatisfaction or possible ambition and is therefore seeking to eliminate them in good time."

The political police was a hotbed of potentially independent "family groups" created at local levels and lifted to Moscow headquarters. The clans were known as "North Caucasians," "Turkestani," "Latvians," and "Caucasians." In 1935, almost 40 of these senior operatives were given high, military-style ranks. Only two would survive the 1937–38 purges. In all, 20,000 security officials were repressed.

Still open to question are the motives behind Stalin's Great Terror. In 1937, entire classes were earmarked for extinction. These included priests, former rich peasants, tsarist officers and criminals – all deemed unlikely to become trustworthy citizens in a time of war. Estimates are that 90,000–100,000 clergy were shot. Soviet novelist Boris Pasternak in his <u>Dr. Zhivago</u> said that the great terror aimed at silencing people from talking about how mistaken Stalin's policy of forced collectivization of the land was. Yale scholar Vernadsky theorized a Party rift in the mid-1930s. He saw Sergei Kirov, Leningrad boss assassinated in 1934, as a new type of leader who was more concerned about practical management issues than ideology. The new generation was said to be more nationalistic than Trotskyite internationalists. The split weakened both sides, and non-party nationalists allegedly looked to non-party circles for support. Vernadsky's implicit conclusion was that Stalin's consolidation of power benefited the economic centralizers and Russian nationalists.

Russian historians in the post-Soviet era opined that policy reasons help to explain why Stalin arrested as spies and terrorists two-thirds of the Bolshevik Central Committee in 1937–38. Leonid Naumov thinks Stalin was angered by doubts that Leninists like Zinoviev and Kamenev should have been shot in 1936. Discord arose too over whether to reach agreement with Nazi Germany over geopolitical issues. The victors approved of more purges and delaying tactics with Hitler, who wanted to deal with a new military leadership in Moscow rather than Stalin. A second opinion is that of K. N. Pisarenko, who sees a divide between Stalin, who wanted contested elections for a new Soviet legislature, and regional Party men, who feared losses in real elections. Stalin dropped the idea of multi-candidate elections and unleashed terror against suspected disloyal citizens; he then decimated the regional barons.

The Kremlin's partner from 1922–33 was another world outcast, the German Republic. The United States denied diplomatic recognition to the Soviet Union until 1933, when Moscow seemed a good counter to Japan. Great Britain worried about Comintern subversion.

A Soviet-German treaty signed at Rapallo in 1922 disavowed mutual war claims and led to restoration of bilateral economic ties. Under secret military accords, German officers trained on unlawful warplanes and tanks inside Russia, and Red Army commanders went to staff colleges in Germany. The Nazi revolution in 1933 cooled relations between the sides. Hitler's anti-Bolshevism was obsessive, and Stalin remained distrustful of the outer world.

As Hitler grew more bellicose, Stalin made an empty defensive alliance with France and Czechoslovakia. The Moscow purges were a factor leading Britain and France to discount the value of the Red Army in a looming clash with Hitler over his designs on Czechoslovakia.

European diplomats in 1938 speculated that Stalin was bringing about dominance of the nationalist element over the Communists in Moscow or Stalin was opportunist, merely concerned with securing his own position. One can infer that Soviet aid shipments to republicans in the Spanish civil war and to Chinese forces opposing Japanese invaders were designed to project an attractive image of the USSR as peace loving.

Ignoring the Russians, British and French leaders met with Hitler and Italian dictator Mussolini at Munich in September 1938. The strongly fortified section of the Czechoslovak frontier that Hitler wanted to annex was surrendered to him. Germany seized the rest of Czechoslovakia in March 1939.

The danger of a war on two fronts threatened both Hitler and Stalin. Russia, Britain, and France might have aligned against Germany or Nazi Germany, and militarist Japan could have attacked Russia, which had fought the Japanese in Outer Mongolia in 1938–39. A third possibility was Soviet neutrality in a new "imperialist" struggle.

Stalin needed time to rebuild his purged officer corps. In a speech to the Party Congress in March 1939, he hinted at suspicion of Britain. Stalin clearly shifted to a pro-Hitler posture in early May 1939. Foreign Commissar Litvinov, a Jew and identified with the half-hearted policy of "collective security," was shelved. Stalin confidant Molotov replaced Litvinov, and the Soviet ambassador and military attaché in Berlin met high Nazis before going to Moscow for discussions.

A Nazi-Soviet nonaggression treaty was signed in August 1939 at the Kremlin. A secret protocol enlarged Soviet western borders roughly to 1914 dimensions. The treaty was to last for 10 years. The NKVD arrested 480,000 in areas allotted to the USSR. A Politburo decree in March 1940 ordered the massacre of over 15,000 prisoners of war taken in the Soviet invasion of eastern Poland in the autumn of 1939.

The Hitler-Stalin pact was shocking to European observers. Rumanian diplomat Grigore Gafencu commented that the Soviets had changed doctrine and principle. Isaac Deutscher, a Polish Marxist, was sure that Lenin would never had made such a deal with an international arsonist like Hitler. But was Lenin's Treaty of Brest-Litovsk in 1918 any less repulsive?

In effect, Stalin served as Hitler's quartermaster. A secret memorandum of the German foreign office, written before Hitler invaded the Soviet Union in June 1941, stated that food and industrial goods from Russia were "a very substantial prop to the German war economy." The Soviet Government sent congratulatory telegrams to Berlin in 1940 after German troops won victories over the Western Allies.

Stalin irked Hitler by annexing the Baltic states and appearing to threaten German oil supplies in Rumania. Hitler started preparations for an invasion of Russia to deprive Britain of hope to win the conflict over mastery of Europe. Driving 400 miles into Soviet territory, the Germany army in the summer of 1941 took a huge toll on the defenders and their material. By October, the Red army had lost over 2 million men; 70–80 percent were captured. At year's end, Soviet weapons losses included 5.5 million rifles; 24,400 artillery pieces; 19,600 tanks and 16,200 aircraft. Stalin had guessed wrongly about Hitler's intentions despite accurate spy reporting.

German occupation policy was brutal. Wholesale food requisitioning was usual in the unreformed collective farms. Many were deported westward as forced laborers. An estimated 2.4 million Jews were killed in German-held areas of the Soviet Union. Historian Peter Longerich has detailed some Nazi mass shootings of Jewish men, women, and children in Russia, Ukraine, Belorussia and Baltic states.

Stalin waged total war, demanding a scorched-earth policy when retreating. Senior party official Nikita Khrushchev pressed for a Soviet attack on Kharkov in May 1942; 18–20 Red Army divisions were destroyed. General Zhukov played a key role in the defense of Moscow (December 1941), and the Stalingrad offensive (November 1942–February 1943). "Where there is Zhukov, there is victory!" became a byword of soldiers. Stalin would demote the popular marshal to outlying garrisons in the post-war period.

Stalin's crash industrialization of the 1930s delivered the goods when needed. Soviet factories in 1943 supplied the Red Army with 4 million rifles and submachine guns, 130,000 artillery systems and 24,000 tanks. U.S. Lend-lease aid came to $9.5 million. The most vital Western shipments were foodstuffs, raw material, locomotives, and heavy trucks, which enabled rapid army mobility in offensives.

Soviet wartime losses were great: 10 million servicemen are thought to have died, 3 million of them prisoners of war. Civilian deaths may have numbered over 15 million. High casualties resulted from the gigantic offensives, Nazi brutalities, and Stalin setting deadlines for the capture of enemy-held towns.

Stalinist crimes committed against people of the western lands, overrun in 1939–40, were horrific. Inside Russia, however, the situation was different during the Nazi-Soviet war. The gap between "us" (society) and "them" (government) narrowed somewhat. Russia was glorified and Bolshevik ideology downplayed. Glorifying Russia meant questioning the choice of socialist development in 1917, a subject of public debate in the Gorbachev years.

Some ethnicities, like the Volga Germans, were repressed during the war, but political nonconformity lasted. A Russian liberal intellectual made a diary entry in November 1941: "…one thinks about the near future. A shift is now underway, and I, along with the others, see much that looks very important. An alliance has been made with the Anglo-Saxon states, the democracies, where the ideas of free thought and religion are deeply embedded structures enabling great economic changes and principles of freedom… Ahead are inevitable basic changes, especially against the backdrop of our victory and that of Anglo-Saxon democracy."

The cheerful outlook of a college professor was registered in an official report filed in 1944 in liberated Kharkov: "Serious changes must occur and indeed are occurring in the country's political life – accord between capitalistic Britain and the USSR, dissolution of the Communist International, separation of schools into boys and girls classes, creation of a Church committee, private trade, and other developments. The changes must and will go further, in particular to democratization of the country's life…" A colleague was overheard saying: "What can be called loosening will occur during the upcoming recovery – personal thoughts, ideas of Western culture, not only in science and technology, but also in morality and politics. Different ways of looking at the world will inevitably begin to seep through to us and basically affect our lives." A Soviet official commented: "Some academics who in the past were inclined to admire Western European institutions and culture fail to understand the nature of the anti-Hitler alliance and are apologists for bourgeois-democratic politics and culture."

That same year in the Urals region, Kadets, and NEP-men were spotted on the horizon. A police agent reported: "Rumors are increasing that soon we will have freedom of different political parties, freedom of private trade, and a new tsar will be elected. America and Britain will lead after the war…" Peasants in the Leningrad region wanted Russia to be a Red-free zone: "After the war, we won't have Communists. The party of Bolsheviks must and will disappear – because our allies Britain and America are capitalists and will do as they see fit."

Deputy security chief Merkulov alerted Party Secretary (for ideology) Zhdanov in October 1944 that anti-Soviet ferment was rising in intellectual circles. A poet was perhaps thinking of the 1825 Decembrists and looked forward to the return of war veterans with new values. A prediction was current that, "after the collapse of Nazi despotism, the democratic world will confront Soviet despotism" and presumably roll it back. Students at the Writers Union institute were rejecting Socialist Realism or prettified images of Soviet life and spawning 'new theories' of the future literature and art. The writers were said to disparage top censor Polikarpov as "stupid and limited…sergeant-major." Long after Stalin died in 1953, purges of alleged wartime collaborators persisted.

In Washington, elites overrated the chances for intimacy with the Kremlin. A War Department memorandum written on the eve of a meeting of British Prime Minister Churchill and U.S. President Roosevelt in August 1943 advised: "Soviet Russia is the decisive factor in the war, she must be given every assurance, and every effort must be made, to obtain her friendship. Since, without question, she will dominate Europe. On the defeat of the Axis, it is even more essential to develop and maintain the most-friendly relations with Russia." FDR's trust of Stalin was voiced in a talk he had with American diplomat William Bullitt in 1943. Bullitt recalled FDR telling him that "I have just a hunch that Stalin doesn't want anything but security for his country, and I think that if I give him everything I possibly can and ask nothing from him in return, Noblesse Oblige, he won't try to annex anything and will work for a world of democracy and peace." The books of FDR's Secretary of Labor Perkins and son Elliott tend to substantiate the recollection of Bullitt.

The realists included U.S. State Department officials present at the Yalta summit of FDR, Stalin, and Churchill in February 1945. They felt that agreements on Poland had to be renegotiated, as too much was conceded to Stalin, who got his versions of Polish borders and legitimacy of the regime created by Soviet forces inside Poland. Churchill too was keenly aware of Stalin's lust of conquest. He tried to save monarchist Greece from Communist revolution by including it in the Western sphere of influence in a plan given to Stalin in October 1944.

There were pendulum swings of British-Soviet dealings in World War II. In 1942, London officials complained that the Russians never reciprocated their confidence over plans or methods. While some felt a gulf between British and Russian mentality rooted in history, they were sure that Churchill's anti-Bolshevik past was a reason for Soviet mistrust. One Englishman was still ambivalent in 1943. He found annoying Soviet secretiveness and suspicion, but Red Army advances were impressive. Allied leaders were angry over Stalin's nasty cables about their failure to attack the German army across the English Channel. Sharp differences arose in 1944 over the makeup of a new Polish government as the Red Army neared Warsaw. By contrast, Foreign Secretary Eden admired Stalin's grasp of military affairs when meeting him in Moscow. In 1945, some were disgusted over Soviet sabotage of agreements reached at Yalta. The apples of discord were Poland, Rumania, United Nations, and the isolation of British prisoners of war freed by Soviet forces in Poland. Eden's private secretary was sure that postwar cooperation with Russia was going to be difficult.

The fears were justified. Stalin told Yugoslav Communist Milovan Djilas in 1944 that Soviet-type regimes would be established wherever the Red Army triumphed. The Kremlin was aiming at maximum security in spite of having subscribed to the principles of the 1941 Atlantic Charter drafted by FDR and Churchill which promised self-rule to nations liberated from Nazism. All told, the land mass of the tsarist empire was restored by Soviet annexations inside Finland, Poland, Rumania, Czechoslovakia and East Prussia. Far Eastern gains at the expense of Japan and China were also notable. The Red

Army would need many divisions – estimated at 175 – to secure the new areas.

Eager for Soviet involvement in his United Nations project, FDR remained conciliatory towards Stalin until his death in April 1945. The new President, Harry Truman, lectured visiting Soviet Foreign Commissar Molotov to keep diplomatic agreements. The stage was set for an outpouring of tough talk inside the U.S. Government. George Kennan, an emotional Foreign Service officer at the Moscow Embassy, in February 1946, sent a telegram to the State Department advising the containment of Communism on a global scale.

Truman invited Churchill to make a policy speech in America deploring the Iron Curtain Moscow had drawn across central European states that it dominated. The former British prime minister called for a military alliance of Western states to deter Soviet aggression. A post-war loan request from Moscow was "lost" at the State Department.

The start of the Cold War may be dated to 1947. Deadlock was reached at the Council of Foreign Ministers where East-West issues were discussed. U.S. Secretary of State Acheson convinced the Senate Foreign Relations Committee that the Soviet Union posed a strategic threat to American interests. Suggestive of Pentagon agitation was an imaginative message that Lt. Gen. Wedemeyer sent to Truman after visiting China, then torn by civil war pitting Communists against Nationalists: "Soviet literature, confirmed repeatedly by Communist leaders, reveals a definite plan for expansion far exceeding that of Nazism in its ambitious scope and dangerous implications." This was an exaggeration. Although esteemed columnist Walter

Lippmann argued against universal containment of Communism, he was uncertain that the Red Army might advance further west.

In 1947, Stalin associate Zhdanov keynoted a rebirth of the Comintern as Communist Information Bureau (Cominform). He resurrected the Leninist "two camps" version of international relations. Czechoslovakia suffered a Communist takeover in 1948, and General Clay, U.S. Commander in West Germany, warned that superpower hostilities could suddenly breakout in Europe. The USSR and U.S. began major rearmament programs. Soviet blockade of West Berlin was defeated by an airlift, and Stalin's prestige dipped. He vented wrath on independent Communists in Yugoslavia, raising fears of Soviet aggression in the Balkans. Communist victory in the Chinese civil war (1949) was viewed in Washington as a Soviet windfall. Assistant Secretary of State for the Far East Rusk heatedly called Red China a "colonial Russian government, a Slavic Manchukuo [Japanese puppet state] on a large scale." He remained hawkish throughout America's war in Vietnam.

Stalin kept to a safe policy of neither war nor peace with America. He approved of a North Korean invasion of the peninsula's pro-U.S. South. But the USSR contributed only advisors and airmen. The Communist side, which was dependent on Chinese troops, lost a million men in the conflict (1950–53).

Inside the USSR, suspected reformers were persecuted. State planner Voznesensky and Party Secretary Kuznetsov were executed as a result of the "Leningrad Case" (1949–50). The creation of Israel in 1948 moved Stalin to fear that

Soviet Jews could develop dual loyalties to the new state and the USSR. David Caute reports: A Politburo edict in February 1949 disbanded associations of Jewish writers and in March Jewish literary critics were expelled from the party and the Jewish theater closed. In May – June 1952, 15 members of the Jewish Anti-Fascist Committee, a Word War II body, were secretly tried, and 13 sentenced to death.

Stalin lacked the vigor to keynote the Party Congress in October 1952. His anti-consumer and anti-peasant gospel remained in force. The personnel changes suggested that younger officials were to be groomed. Stalin told a secret panel that he wished to be relieved of the top Party job, but henchmen suspected a ruse to smoke-out enemies, and begged the leader to stay at the helm, which he did. A "Doctors' Case," announced in 1953, featured the arrest of Kremlin physicians for plotting to murder Soviet leaders. The public feared medical terrorism. Stalin's death in March forestalled a new purge.

Soviet society was ailing from self-isolation and over-investment in arms industries. Bread shortages were common, and many workers lived in hated barracks. Managerial initiative was stifled, and minimal contacts with the West impeded the introduction of new technology. The tight censorship alienated writers, and legality was rare. New U.S. President Eisenhower might have escalated the Sino-American war over Korea.

Stalin's heirs nullified the Doctors' Case and urged coexistence of the superpowers. Churchill, again prime minister, wanted to make an exploratory visit to Moscow; Eisenhower rejected the bid, as did the British Foreign

Office. A Kremlin scheme to seduce the West Germans was feared in Washington and London.

Soviet leader Khrushchev reached the peak of Kremlin authority in a series of internal clashes:

1. Security chief Beria was ousted in June 1953. He pressed for legality and the promotion of more non-Russians to posts in the borderlands.
2. Premier Malenkov fell in January 1955, accused of neglecting heavy industries.
3. Foreign Minister Molotov erred by opposing an Austrian peace treaty and lost his post.
4. A trio of cautious men was ousted in June 1957 over economic management issues.
5. Marshal Zhakov was shelved in October 1957 as "inclined to adventurism." Khrushchev initiated limited reforms, easing food, and housing crises. A "secret speech" that Khrushchev made in 1956 debunked the Stalin myth and rocked the Soviet orbit. Why the dethronement of Stalin? Some thought the action was meant to expedite the release of political prisoners from harsh labor camp conditions. Others believed that Khrushchev wished to discredit formulas that blocked the adoption of new methods of governance. A faction-fighting theory is that Stalin was debunked to undermine archconservatives within the Stalin clique who were still influential.

A worker revolt over sudden price rises in June 1962 hit the south Russian town of Novocherkassk; many protesters were slain, and death sentences meted out. Khrushchev was ousted in October 1964 for exerting too much pressure on administrators.

New Party head Leonid Brezhnev mixed coercion of intellectuals with tolerance of vast corruption. A wartime political officer, he was fond of medals, uniforms, and veterans' reunions. Hunting and a collection of foreign cars were pastimes. What he hated were Maoists and native dissidents. Intellectual rebels were confined to asylums for "reformist delusions." A doctrine of limited sovereignty of USSR-aligned states was approved in 1968 after the Soviet Army suppressed a reform Communist movement in Czechoslovakia. Gordon Barrass, a former British official, heard from a Kremlin speechwriter that Moscow's forward Africa policy in the 1970s was driven by the feeling that an empire was the attribute of a great power.

A backstage critic of Brezhnev was Alexander Shelepin. Born in 1918, he was a college graduate and rose to head the Young Communist League. Shelepin gained the KGB chairmanship and got a seat at the Party Secretariat. He espoused "triple" vigilance and was suddenly demoted to trade union head in 1967, apparently for opposing Brezhnev's handling of the latest Middle East crisis.

In Brezhnev's time, a few Western observers detected signs of Soviet decay. Jacob Beam, U.S. Chief of Mission in Moscow, underlined ethnic tensions in the Baltics, Western Ukraine, and North Caucasus. He correctly predicted that nationality discord would accompany future systemic change. Also perceptive, German analyst Wolfgang Leonhard was persuaded that the Soviet polity was weakening.

Brezhnev loyalists directed an interregnum from his death in 1982 to the advent of 54-year-old Mikhail Gorbachev as Party General Secretary in 1985. Over the next six years, he charted a course between reactionaries and radical reformers. "New Thinking" about foreign affairs marked a retreat from the stance of Soviet dominance over East Europe.

Gorbachev bid for public support, illuminating a disaster at the nuclear power plant in the Ukrainian town of Chernobyl. He visited provinces and sent public grievances to top Party men. A number of banned books, films, and plays were released to discredit abusers of power.

NEP theorists were acclaimed, and some allowance was made for independence of factory managers, cooperatives, and private businesses. Quashing of the fabricated case made against onetime anti-Stalinists in 1938 undermined extant hardliners.

Gorbachev initiated elections with alternative candidates for Party and state posts. A raucous Congress of People's Deputies was held, and rival platforms surfaced. Russian populist Boris Yeltsin and dissident Andrey Sakharov starred at the forum.

Gorbachev's relaxed foreign policy was to secure Western loans to compensate for a sharp drop in world oil prices. The plunge was costing Moscow $20 billion a year. A peace program included endorsing universal human values and unilateral reduction of Soviet armed forces – steps toward a "new world order." Watchful waiting was the official American response. The White House expected full marketization of the Soviet economy before granting credits to the USSR.

Gorbachev faltered, as high officials increasingly opposed changes and many below were passive. Clubs of reform-minded citizens failed to connect "them" and "us." One Soviet journalist compared the people-elites relationship to an impotent man on top of a frigid woman.

The last straw for hardliners was Gorbachev's move to federalize the multinational Soviet state. A coup was hatched in August 1991 and defeated thanks to Yeltsin, who, as Russian Federation president, sprung his own coup to sweep away both Gorbachev and the USSR. The victors scoffed at the Gorbachevites: "The myopic policy of the center led to a deep economic and political crisis, the collapse of production, a catastrophic lowering of the living standard of practically all strata of society… The growth of social tension and in many regions of the former USSR led to inter-ethnic conflicts with great loss of life." Gorbachev was more balanced in a televised farewell speech to the nation. He was proud to have introduced freedoms of elections, press, and religion; boosted private farming; and ended the Cold War. Blame for the collapse of the USSR was cast on the defective political culture of citizens and the botched reactionary coup of the summer of 1991. Thus, Gorbachev implied that public apathy and elite plotting, rather than legislative impeachment, had brought him down.

In a memoir, Gorbachev did not join foreign critics who cast blame on the "ideocratic" Communist Party for Soviet misrule. Deplored are habit, the military, and secret police. Gorbachev denounced, too, the negative influence of Russian leaders' centuries-old craving to dominate neighbors. The custom was said to evoke fears of again becoming wards of Moscow. The Soviet Defense Ministry is hit for never proposing cuts in arms spending. And KGB chief Shelepin is denounced for sending a memorandum to Khrushchev advising the destruction of documents attesting to an NKVD massacre of Polish officers and civilians in 1940.

The sentimental reviewer of a Gorbachev biography depicts the former leader as virtually Tsar Mikhail the Good. In reality, Gorbachev was a combative innovator who, with a policy of loosening the screws, gambled with the public interest. He clashed with rival power groups in a five-sided brawl:

1. Gorbachev – Reformist
2. Yegor Ligachev – Neo-Stalinist
3. Yeltsin – Centrist
4. Republic-level bosses – Autonomists
5. Army and police – Guardians of Order

Alliances were shifting, and Yeltsin was a wild card.

Analysts will diverge over Gorbachev's personal thinking, which reminds one of Napoleon I or Lenin – "Commit yourself and see!" How far would the unbinding of society be allowed? Was the Communist Party to become a European-style Social Democratic force? Did Gorbachev expect U.S. President George W. Bush to offer the USSR a Marshall Plan?

The smoke over Soviet ruins would not begin to clear for a decade.

Note on Post-Soviet Russia

After Gorbachev, Yeltsin led a Russian state of managed chaos. He ruled largely by presidential decree after an armed factional clash at the parliament. Elections soon showed a tilt in favor of stricter conservatism.

Vladimir Putin, as strongman of the Russian Federation since 2000, was worrisome to Western leaders. He came of age under Brezhnev, imperial power politician and nemesis of dissidents. A former KBG officer, Putin's worldview was conservative nationalist. Bureaucratic lords and vassals once more prevailed. A new class of tycoons emerged, as did Mafia-type gangs.

The State was put back in control of economic firms; private ownership before Putin had risen to 70 percent of all firms. That much of the whole was returned to the State. Kremlin insiders were divided over the shift back to more State dominance. One free marketer was imprisoned on corruption charges. Stalinist "show trials" of the 1930s were recalled in legal circles. Old wine in old bottles? Similarly, the secret police were reportedly eager to use falsified evidence to stifle dissidents.

"Youth army" was a patriotic echo of the introduction of military drill in Russian high schools after liberal revolutions in Europe during 1848. Russia scholar Rachel Polonsky cites "racial supremacist tracts" glorifying Putin as energetic and patriotic.

A second Chechen war subdued rebels in that restive province of the Caucasus. Protest demonstrations were suppressed. Independent organizations were restricted under Putin's slogan of "sovereign democracy." Naturally enough, Putin warned against demonizing Stalin.

The U.S. was accused of championing regime change, that is, subversion of unfriendly states. Imperial decline was lamented in the formula that Soviet collapse was a geopolitical disaster. Like the USSR, Russia was willing to partner with rogue regimes like North Korea.

Expansionism was again in vogue. Russia annexed two provinces in Georgia, and Crimea in Ukraine. Russian citizenship was illegally imposed on Crimean peoples, and critics of the regime severely punished. Military power was projected by intervention in the Syrian civil war. The aggressiveness moved NATO to deploy small troop units to the Baltics and Poland. A U.S. general later said that Putin had become coup-proof. But that remained to be seen in light of the new Russian unpredictability. NATO allies were alarmed by signs that Russian agents had poisoned a former Soviet intelligence officer living in Britain. U.S. officials accused Russia of having grand designs of dominating Europe.

It seemed unlikely, however, that Putin would mellow and agree to ease superpower tensions. He appeared to belong to a diehard school of thought. Wishing to "show teeth" or challenge American swagger.

In any event, youths in St. Petersburg, Putin's hometown, soon demonstrated with chants of "Putin – Thief!" Was the Leader concerned that angry hackers might delve into his personal financial affairs? That same October 2017, Putin spoke to his Security Council and warned "the level of threat in the informational space is on the rise." He attacked "persons and groups using the Internet for criminal purposes." Riot police were rough with anti-Putin youths.

With frosty remarks, Putin attended the unveiling in Moscow of a bronze monument to honor victims of unlawful political repression during the Soviet era. The gesture may have been made for Putin to bank goodwill as a humanist. Intellectual critics derided Putin's maneuvering.

In 2017, a crackdown on foreign media inside Russia was sensed after a new law was enacted requiring some Western news outlets to register with authorities as "foreign agents." The ominous label signaled to home audiences an official warning not to fraternize with snooping aliens.

Our best surmise is that the bond between rulers and subjects was strengthened by shows of Russian military power in Georgia, Ukraine, and Syria. Those displays of muscle seem to have increased pride among most citizens. Elite confidence was no doubt bolstered, too, when China's president reaffirmed the rebirth of a strategic partnership with Russia. Putin hinted that his goal was to build a new Russian empire. War, Revolution, or Fratricide – defining features of Russian history – could thwart his ambitions.

Conclusions

Is Russia a hopeless case, fated to endure the Leviathan State and bullying dictators? The historical record warns against dream scenarios. Neither oil prices nor political legacy are necessarily crucial factors in Kremlin policy making. Russian character is very important and favors the likelihood of continuity over change in the near term. Acute crisis has hugely shaped Russian mentality. This was the case with the Mongol conquest (13th century) Time of Troubles (17th century), 1812 and Nazi-Soviet war (1941–45). Social-political process was viewed in terms of strong leadership, discipline, and ethnicity. National traditions as taught at universities were "inviolable."

Just as firmly embedded in the Russian consciousness is the expectation of arbitrary power (proizvol). In Western Europe, towns were strongholds of judicial principles. Russian cities were burned in the Mongol onslaught. Unknown to villagers were such legalisms as habeas corpus or a writ to bring a party before a court. The aristocratic Lord was judge and jury until serfdom was ended in 1861. Revolutionary instinct since 1917 replaced noble privilege in the dispensing of justice.

The Russian is distrustful of spontaneity, and to curb it will try counter-productive measures. Weakness of lower governing bodies inspired Empress Elizabeth (reigned 1741–62) to centralize all authority. At the dawn of the 20th century a newspaper complained of "almost complete absence of economic independence" in industry and advised that "the complex and delicate mechanism of industrial development cannot be administered from one single center." Stalin's heirs agreed but clung to the leader's command-administrative system, which many saw as root cause of goods shortages and corruption. The system was a copy of the German model of World War I and unrelated to the Communist ideology that some foreigners wrongly viewed as Soviet lodestar.

Caution has long been a Russian compulsion. Tsarist backwardness compelled Nicholas II to pursue moderation after his 1905 defeat by underrated Japan. Heedful of the weakness of the new Red Army, Lenin in 1918 waged a bitter fight to defang the Revolutionary War faction in the Bolshevik leadership. Stalin and Khrushchev retreated in crises over Berlin and Cuba, respectively.

Naivety and devoutness are age-old phenomena. Until 1783 rumors swirled that another pretender to the throne was alive and on a rampage. Now millions attend exhibits of saintly relics, delivering appeals for miracle-working assistance. The Russian president is there, vigorously crossing himself. As a television viewer the Russian wants discussions to end in unanimity (edinoglasie), an Orthodox Church virtue.

The Russian's heart rate spikes, watching his nation's soldiers on parade. From the 1200s on, the Moscow state expanded by force of arms. Courage, endurance, and stoicism were usual on the battlefield. Hero cults glorified the captains Suvorov, Kutuzov, and Zhukov. All this was effectively a vote for a policy of strength. Public opinion can bolster elite standing even in autocratic polities. Sentimental pacifism has indeed made little headway in a society so often riven by war.

Stalin, over a span of nearly 30 years, played the role of master of the Russian political mind. His slogan of "Socialism in One Country" won him popularity among the Bolshevik Party faithful, who loathed the likes of Trotsky and Zinoviev – Jewish internationalists – who competed for the Lenin succession. All rejected old-school honor and dignity but the Stalinists, as civil war front liners, would prove to be savage.

Under Stalin, politics kept primacy over economics. The race to attain military parity with the Great Powers was sent into high gear, and the death toll of famine and state terror was huge. After Stalin, elite pressure led to Khrushchev's half-reforms and Gorbachev's bolder steps to remedy system decay were halted to end still more chaos.

In 2053 a century will have passed since the death of the "dread father," as one poet called the last of revolutionary-despots. It is conceivable that around that time Russian progressives may have garnered the social support to take strong action for representative government and civil rights. The incipient signs of generational unrest should be recognized. Some youngsters currently doubt the legitimacy of state-run firms that Putin's regime favors. The formation of a new militarized youth movement hints at cracks in the time-honored mold of blind obedience and patriotic fervor. The prospects for world peace would brighten if old- fashioned but persistent Russian militarism abated in the wake of a democracy upsurge. On the other hand, one must keep in mind that historically the Russian military has been influential, allying with social groups which agree that national existence has often depended on vitality of the country's armed forces.

In the meantime, new visions of the Russian past can be expected from the nation's historians. The historical-judicial and historical-economic schools have gazed at legal and production dynamics, respectively. A State school was the creation of Moscow liberal professor Boris Chicherin (1828–1904). It highlighted the top-down binding and unbinding of social classes over the span of four centuries. The Eurasian model was a work of Russian emigres in the 1920s. It claims that the motherland belongs to a cultural formation that lays between a hostile China and no more friendly Western civilization.

Chicherin's overview of social group binding and unbinding is relatable to the Soviet and post-totalitarian experience of Russians.

Chronology

988	Baptism of Vladimir and Russia's conversion to Orthodoxy
1147	First written mention of Moscow
1169	Sack of Kiev by Bogoliubsky
1237–1482	Mongols dominate Russia
1376	Metropolitan established in Moscow
1393	Nizhny Novgorod annexed by Moscow Grand Prince
1432–50	Civil war over Moscow Grand Princedom
1471	Marriage of tsar lvan III with Sophia Palaiologos of Byzantium
1547	lvan the Terrible crowned tsar
1565–72	Ivan's reign of terror
1589	Moscow Patriarchate created
1598	Boris Godunov elected tsar by national assembly
1613	Mikhail Romanov elected tsar by national assembly
1654	Church schism begins; Ukraine unites with Muscovy
1694	Peter takes over government
1703	St. Petersburg founded

1721	Patriarchate abolished and State's Holy Synod created
1730–40	Rise and fall of German tyrant Biron
1755	Moscow University founded
1762	Tsar Peter III murdered
1762–96	Catherine the Great reigns
1773–5	Pugachov revolt
1783	Crimea annexed
1801	Tsar Paul murdered
1812	Napoleon I fails to conquer Russia
1816	Secret officer societies emerge
1825	Decembrist revolt
1835	Code of Laws
1849	Nicholas I suppresses revolution in Hungary
1853–6	Crimean War
1861	Serfs freed
1863	Polish rebellion
1864	Local government reforms
1867	Alaska sold to U.S.A.
1881	Alexander II assassinated
1891	Trans-Siberian railroad begins; famine
1894	Alliance with France
1904–5	Russo-Japanese war
1905	Revolution, October Manifesto promises political and civil rights
1906	First Duma
1906–11	Stolypin premier and agrarian reform
1907	Alliance with Britain
1914–18	World War I

1917	Revolution, Nicholas II abdicates, Provisional Government, Bolshevik coup
1918	Brest-Litovsk peace treaty with German alliance, Russia losses Baltics, Ukraine, Bessarabia
1918–20	Civil and Polish wars
1919	Communist International founded
1921	New Economic Policy, Kronstadt revolt
1922	Soviet-German Treaty of Rapallo, 11 Moscow churchmen condemned to death
1923	USSR constitution adopted
1924	Lenin dies, triumvirate rules
1927	Stalin expels rivals from Kremlin
1929	Five-year plans and farm collective drive really begin, 115 academics arrested on political grounds
1930	48 food industry scientists arrested and shot
1933	US recognizes USSR
1934	Politburo member Kriov assassinated
1935	USSR admitted to League of Nations, treaties with France and Czechoslovakia
1936–8	New USSR constitution, Great Terror, Moscow trials of Old Bolsheviks
1939	Soviet-German treaty, World War II, Red Army occupies eastern Poland
1939–40	Soviet-Finnish war, USSR expelled from League of Nations
1940	Baltic states, Bessarabia, and Northern Bukovina annexed in USSR

1941	Soviet-Japanese neutrality pact, Germany invades USSR
1943	Red Army wins at Stalingrad and Kursk
1944	German east front collapses
1945	Germany defeated, Soviet war dead at 27 million
1947–89	Cold War: US-USSR rivalry over geopolitical threats
1950	Senior Kremlin leaders shot over "Leningrad case"
1953	Kremlin doctors arrested, Stalin dies, political police tribunal abolished
1956	Party head Khrushchev denounces Stalin era crimes
1962	Cuban missile crises, Novocherkassk rioting over food prices
1964	Brezhnev replaces Khrushchev in coup
1985–2000	Gorbachev reforms, Yeltsin disarray, Putin conservatism begins

Bibliography

Action, E. and Stableford, T., The Soviet Union. A Documentary History. 2 Vols. (Exeter: 2005 and 2007).

Albertini, L., The Origins of the War of 1914. 3 Vols. (London: 2014).

Barrass, G. S., The Great Cold War – A Journey Through the Hall of Mirrors. (Stanford: 2009).

Chamberlain, L., Lenin's Private War – The Voyage of the Philosophy Steamer and the Exile of The Intelligentsia. (New York: 2007).

Chamberlain, L., Motherland – A Philosophical History of Russia. (New York: 2007).

Crankshaw, E., Russia Without Stalin – The Emerging Pattern. (New York: 1956).

Curtis, W.E., The Land of the Nihilist. Russia: Its People, Its Places, Its Politics. A Narrative of Travel in the Czar's Domions. (Chicago: 1888).

Darrilov, V.P., "Stalinizm I Sovetskoe Obshchestvo," 50 *let bez Stalina*. (Moscow: 2005).

Documents on German Foreign Policy 1918–1945. (London: 1983).

Emmons, Terence, ed. and translator, Time of Troubles: The Diary of Iurii Vladimirovich Got'e. Moscow, July 8, 1917 to July 23, 1922. (Princeton: 1988).

Florinsky, M. T., Russia: A History and an Interpretation. 2 Vols. (New York: 1955).

Gilbert, M., The First World War – A Complete History. (New York: 1994).

Gorbachev, M. S., Memoirs. (New York: 1995).

Hartman, Christian Operation Barbarossa – Nazi Germany's War in the East 1941–1945. (Oxford: 2013).

Harvey, J., ed., The War Diaries of Oliver Harvey – 1941–1945. (London: 1978).

Karamzin, N.M., Istariia Gosudavstva Rossiiskogo. 3 Vols. (Moscow: 2007).

Kennedy, P.M. The Rise and Fall of the Great Powers – Economic Change and Military Conflict from 1500 to 2000. (New York: 1987).

Kliuchevsky, V. 0., Russkaia istoriia. (Moscow: 2008).
Kornilov, A. A., Kurs istorii Rossii XIX veka. (Moscow: 2004).

Leonhard, W., "Are We Moving Toward a Post-Communist Era? The Soviet Empire in Crisis," Encounter. (London, November 1980).

Lippmann, W., The Cold War – A Study in U.S. Foreign Policy. (New York: 1972).

Manning, R. T., The Crisis of the Old Order in Russia – Gentry and Government. (Princeton: 1982).

Mawdsley, E., The Stalin Years: The Soviet Union.1929–1953. (Manchester: 2001).

Mawdsley, E., Thunder in the East: The Nazi-Soviet War. 1941–1945. (London: 2005).

Mawdsley, E., The Russian Civil War. (New York: 2007).

Maynard, J., Russia In Flux. (New York: 1948).

Medvedev, R. A. and Medvedev, Zh. A., The Unknown Stalin – His Life, Death, and Legacy. (Woodstock: 2003).

Mesissner, B., "Gorbachev's Perestroika: Reform or Revolution?" Aussenpolitik. Vol. 38, No, 3. (1987).

Molotov, Malenkov, Kaggnovich, Stenogramma iunskogo plenuma TsK. KPSS. 1957. (Moscow:1998).
Namier, L. B., Diplomatic Prelude 1938–1939. (London: 1948).

Naumov, L. Stalin i NKVD. (Moscow: 2007).

Pares, B. The Fall of the Russian Monarchy – A Study of Evidence. (New York: 1961).

Platonov, S. F. Lektsii po Russkoi istsorii. (Moscow: 1993).

Riasanovsky, N. V. A History of Russia. (New York: 1993).

Riha, Thomas, Readings in Russian Civilization. 3 Vols (Chicago: 1969).

Seton-Watson, H. The Russian Empire 1801–1917. (Oxford: 1990).

Sumner, B. H. A Short History of Russia. (New York: 1943).

Taylor, A. J. The Struggle for Mastery in Europe 1848–1918. (Oxford: 1954).

Vernadsky, G. Russkaia istoriia. (Moscow: 2001).

Ward, C. The Stalinist Dictatorship. (London: 1998).

Wilmot, C. The Struggle for Europe. (Chatham: 1997).